KU-175-169

KYLE

A Mother's Love in Action

VICTOR MAXWELL
with
ALISON SHIELDS

KYLE - A MOTHER'S LOVE IN ACTION
© 2007 Victor Maxwell

All rights reserved

No part of this book may be reproduced, stored in a retrieval system,
or transmitted in any form or by any means - electronic, mechanical, photocopy,
recording or otherwise - without written permission of the publisher, except for
brief quotation in written reviews.

First published October 2007

ISBN   0 9551545 2 9

JC Print Ltd., Belfast
Telephone: 07860 205333
Fax: 028 9079 0420

KYLE

A Mother's Love in Action

How This Book Came About

On the day before our son Kyle died our family had gathered at his bedside at the Children's Hospice in Newtownabbey. Our Pastor, Alan Dundas, from Kilkeel Baptist Tabernacle, spent most of that day and right through the next night with us. During Kyle's final hours I was looking over the journal that I had kept during the ten years since our darling boy had been diagnosed. In a moment of impulse I offered the journal to Pastor Dundas for his perusal. I did not know then what that moment of impulse would lead to.

At Kyle's funeral service three days later Pastor Dundas made mention of several observations from that journal. Subsequently, Alan and many others friends suggested that I should write a book based on the journal I had kept. They said it would be of great benefit to others. To be perfectly honest, when I considered this suggestion I felt totally inadequate to even contemplate trying to write a book. Besides never having written anything before, I wondered how I could ever open up my heart to share all the roller-coaster of those intimate and personal emotions I had experienced. Furthermore, I wondered where I would even begin and doubted if anyone would be interested in reading it anyway.

A few weeks later I was reading my Bible and came to Jeremiah 30:2; "Thus speaketh the Lord God of Israel saying, write all the words that I have spoken unto thee in a book." It stopped me in my tracks and I had to read the words again, "...write all the words that I have spoken unto thee in a book." That seemed clear enough, even though I was still very hesitant.

Victor Maxwell was one of those who on hearing about the journal, encouraged me to think of putting pen to paper, or my fingers to a keyboard, to put something in print. He said that besides helping others, it might be good therapy for me. I had read Victor's book, *Handling Hot Potatoes*, and it had been a real source of help to me during those difficult years when I was caring for our special-needs boy. After these promptings and encouragements, I felt that my few thoughts and experiences just might be a blessing or help to others.

I have, therefore, jotted down these notes, recalling a lot of painful, happy and amusing memories. In retrospect, I have to say that writing this book has been a great help to me. It has been very beneficial to recall and work through how God has helped our family in the good times and through the difficult days.

I trust this book will be a blessing and help to you.

KYLE

A Mother's Love in Action

THANKS

I wish to thank the following people for their contribution to this book:

Thank you to S. McConnell & Sons of Kilkeel. Your support in funding this book is very much appreciated.

I have to thank our pastor, Alan Dundas. I guess if you had never mentioned my journal at Kyle's Funeral Service this book would never have materialised. As a family we will always be grateful for the pastoral love, sincerity, consideration and caring support which you showed to us. We thank God for the part you and Heather have had in our lives. We pray that God will continue to bless your ministry in Kilkeel Baptist Tabernacle and that you will have many more blessed years with us.

Victor, thank you for working extremely hard in piecing this book together. It has been a privilege to work with someone so gracious and talented.

Wilma, you have been a tremendous help in the preparation of this book. Your advice and encouragement have been extremely useful.

Andrew, thank you for being a wonderful husband; for understanding me, loving me and being there to support me. Even when I have been engrossed in writing at 4.00 am, you were there to remind me that I needed my sleep if I expected to function during the next day.

Most of all I have to thank Almighty God who has blessed me with all spiritual blessings in heavenly places in Christ. Thank you God for giving us Kyle and for the privilege of being his parents for a few short years. Your grace and power has sustained us through the darkest hours. Andrew and I can say from our hearts, "The Lord gave, and the Lord hath taken away; blessed be the name of the Lord."

Alison Shields

1

Life is a Scramble

The weather forecast for Ulster's north coast was for a bright and breezy Easter Monday in April 2006. Andrew, my husband, knew that caravaners and families would be heading to the various resorts and spectacular beaches that make this area of amazing natural beauty so popular. In order to avoid the almost inevitable tedious traffic delays next morning, Andrew and our sons, Craig and Scott, left our home near Kilkeel just before midnight on Sunday. Meanwhile, I stayed at home to look after our youngest son, Kyle, and looked forward to enjoying a few quiet days over Easter.

The reason for Andrew and our boys travelling north was not the attraction of surfing or swimming on the rolling breakers of the North Atlantic. Craig had another pursuit in mind. In the back of their white motocross van, in which they travelled, were two motor cycles, a 250F Kawasaki scrambler and a 125cc Kawasaki. Craig was intending to compete at the two-day motocross event at Ballykelly in County Londonderry on Easter Monday and Tuesday. Scott had no plans to ride as he was still suffering from a sprained wrist, gained as a consequence of falling off his pushbike on Saturday while trying to do some teenage stunts.

Craig and Scott were following the same interests and hobby as Andrew had indulged in many years earlier. In fact, Andrew even conceded to me that the boys were probably better at this rough-riding sport over humpback hills and torturous ploughed-up courses than he had ever been. So keen were our sons in their hobby that they were prepared to sleep overnight in the back of the specially-adapted van before the track event next day. Furthermore, I was very content to see our boys enjoy their sporting interests with Andrew, just as fathers and sons ideally do.

This trip was no different. Andrew phoned me the following morning to say that after two and a half-hours on the road they had finally bedded down in the rear of the van in the wee hours of Monday morning. It was a short night, but the adrenaline was already flowing when they stirred from their sleep to discover that it was a dry and bright morning. After some breakfast Craig and Scott were pleased to meet up with several of their competitors and friends from the scrambling fraternity. Apparently, Craig had won their respect as a competent challenger at other motocross events.

Later on Andrew filled me in on the events that followed that day. He explained that after unloading the scramblers from the back of the vehicle and going through the formality of registration, Craig had donned his colourful racing outfit while he warmed up the bike. Once astride the scrambler Craig opened the throttle with an ear-piercing roar from the engine and sped off for a closer inspection of the undulating course. The ground was firm and the course seemed to be in excellent condition. After a good ride in his grade during practice Craig had qualified for the championship event. He expressed to Andrew how he had been eagerly looking forward to this first race.

Eventually Roy Neill, the race commentator, called all competitors to the starting line. The pitch of reverberating engines and the smell of exhaust fumes from forty rip-roaring scrambler engines filled the air. When the starting gates dropped the challengers sped off toward the first tight right-hand bend. Craig got off to a brilliant start and had positioned himself into fifth place as they exited the bend.

As usual, Andrew had located a good vantage point from where he hoped to have a good view of Craig coming airborne over the first few jumps. Craig was still in fifth place as the bikes dropped downhill and disappeared from view for a few seconds. When the riders emerged again Andrew counted the bikes one by one to see if Craig had managed to hold his position. He was puzzled when the first group of riders came through and there was no sign of Craig. He glanced across the track and noticed the yellow flags being waved indicating that a rider had come off. All sorts of thoughts filled Andrew's mind, *Is it Craig? Has he collided? Is he hurt?*

Within seconds the stewards raised a medical flag to alert the paramedics that their assistance was urgently required at the scene of an accident. Instinctively Andrew knew he had to make his way to the other side of the hill as quickly as possible to find out what had happened and if the incident involved Craig.

Andrew and Scott were surprised to find Craig lying prostrate on the grass near to his machine with several stewards around him. "It's a broken leg," one of the stewards said to Andrew. "His machine flipped into the air and he came off. It's a mercy the bike didn't fall on top of him."

Some paramedics had been nearby and were on the scene very promptly. They immobilised Craig's leg until an ambulance arrived to transport him to Altnagelvin Hospital in Londonderry. Andrew's friends told him to head on over to the hospital while they and Scott would take care of Craig's gear. Instead of Andrew driving the twelve miles to the hospital a friend of Craig's offered to take him. They set off in such hot pursuit of the ambulance that they arrived there before Craig.

It was on his way to the hospital that Andrew called me on his mobile phone. He knew that I would be at home with Kyle who needed round-the-clock care and attention. I was used to Andrew calling and giving me updates on the boys' progress throughout the day, but on this occasion

I was stunned to hear of the mishap. I immediately began to plan how I would be able to travel to Londonderry to see Craig, but I also knew that before I could go anywhere I would have to organise care for Kyle.

I phoned the Belfast Children's Hospice only to learn that they could not accommodate Kyle until Wednesday. This meant that I would be unable to see Craig for another forty-eight hours. Andrew called back a little later to inform me that Craig's leg was definitely broken and the surgeons intended to operate the following day. I felt so frustrated for I wanted to drop everything and rush to Craig's bedside, but with no one to care for Kyle I could not split myself in two or be in two places at the same time.

Besides my own frustration, I knew Craig would be looking for me so I tried other avenues to provide a carer for Kyle. However, I knew this would be difficult for most people would have already made their plans for the Easter holiday weekend. God answered prayer and I was finally able to find a carer for Tuesday evening so Andrew drove all the way from Londonderry to Kilkeel, collected me and together we returned to Altnagelvin Hospital.

On our arrival we were informed that Craig's surgery had been delayed until Wednesday. I was not unduly concerned for I was so glad to see Craig and be able to allay some of my fears and worries. After spending several hours with Craig we had to return to Kilkeel to relieve the carer who was looking after Kyle. Before leaving I assured Craig that I would return the next day and would be there for him when he came out of theatre.

Mum and Dad travelled with me to Londonderry the following day. The trip took almost three hours since we had to make a detour to leave Kyle at the Children's Hospice as previously arranged. The long journey gave me time to reflect on all that had happened and how it would affect our family for the next week. I thought to myself that a couple of trips to Londonderry had not been part of my plans for Easter. However, as a mother of two teenage boys, I was aware that coping with accidents was an occupational hazard, especially when their hobbies included motocross and quad bike riding.

To be truthful, I was not unduly worried about Craig for I had convinced myself that it was only a broken leg and I knew that surgery for this was fairly common. I was more concerned about the inconvenience caused by Craig's accident having happened at far-off Ballykelly and being hospitalised in Londonderry which is well over a hundred miles away from our home in Kilkeel.

Being so far from home meant it was unlikely that Craig would have many visitors, so I was pleased that I would be able to stay at the hospital for a few days and provide some company for him. Furthermore, I knew that even seventeen-year-old sons want their Mum when they are frightened and in pain. I had also calculated that Craig might be in Altnagelvin Hospital for five days or maybe even a week at the most, before he would be allowed back home where everything would settle back into its normal routine again.

I expected Craig to be coming out of theatre just about the time we would arrive and thought it would be nice for him to see his Mum when he came round from the anaesthetic in the recovery suite. However, not only was Craig still in theatre when we arrived, we were also told that he could be there for at least another hour. I said my goodbyes to Mum and Dad who had decided to head back to Kilkeel. I felt there was little point in them hanging around in the waiting area of the hospital indefinitely seeing that they had such a long drive back home. Besides, Craig would likely be very drowsy for several hours after his operation.

After Mum and Dad left, I settled down in a chair on the ward which had been allocated to Craig. In the quietness I took time to pray that everything would go well for Craig in theatre and that he would make a speedy recovery. As I was meditating and praying I became aware of someone approaching.

"Mrs Shields?" the man asked

I nodded in affirmation

"I'm Mr..." I did not catch the name. "I've just come from theatre and we could not put the pin in Craig's leg. We had to abort the operation and they are taking your son to intensive care. Someone will be along shortly to take you down. Craig has developed a fat embolism."

My mind whirled. This was definitely not in my plans. As I waited for this "someone" to come for me, I recalled another occasion when I had entered a hospital and was left with news that totally shook my world.

Let me tell you how it all began.

Craig in action

"Frightening circumstances are less troublesome when we can trust the hands that control them" (Alison's Journal).

2

Rough and Tumble Days

I am a little bit biased, but I think there is no more beautiful place in the whole of Ireland than the region known as "the Kingdom of Mourne." I was privileged to be born in this idyllic and picturesque part of Ulster. Here in this region of outstanding natural beauty the rocky coastline of County Down sweeps up to meet the steep and dark Mountains of Mourne. The distinctive peaks of Slieve Donard, Slieve Croob, Big Binnian and Wee Binnian stand tall on the sky-line and from the elevation of their slopes and summits the climber has breathtaking views across the patchwork of the fertile countryside with its "forty shades of green". As the gaze falls downward it might settle on the dark, still waters of the Silent Valley which provides a large part of Northern Ireland with its water supply. In the distance the climber can also see the busy fishing port of Kilkeel and the Victorian resort of Rostrevor hugging the shore. Beyond the coastline, the Irish Sea rises to meet the azure of the sky on the distant horizon with faint glimpses of the Isle of Man on a clear day.

Kilkeel has always been my home. I was born there before the cruel atrocities of "the Troubles" ever stained the history of Northern Ireland. Our local "clan" bears one of the more familiar names in the Kingdom of Mourne, McConnell, and to this name my parents added my first name, Alison. Even though I am a twin, I was always looked upon as the youngest of the three McConnell girls in our home. Wilma was only thirteen months old when we were born. With her limited vocabulary at that age she referred to the two additions to her family as "the doggies."

For many years my sister, Eunice, took great delight in referring to me as the baby of the family, even though she arrived into the world just a few minutes ahead of me. When we were younger I did not like being called the youngest sister, however, now that we are older the tables have turned to my advantage and I am only too glad to own the distinction of being the youngest of the McConnell sisters.

With three lively and energetic daughters there was never a dull moment in our home. During our adolescent years we were not unduly exposed to the political upheaval and terrorist onslaughts which wreaked havoc across other parts of Ulster. In the surrounding countryside we saw police and army patrols. Several local men had been killed, periodically we heard about bomb blasts in Belfast, ambushes in the countryside and assassinations of security officers. We even experienced several bomb alerts at our school, but these were usually attributed to the fifth-formers wanting some time out of class. However, we were pretty good at creating enough trouble of our own. Tucked away in the heart of the Mournes we considered our lives to be quite normal, carefree and somewhat sheltered.

Not only was our home-life quite sheltered, it was also strict. My sisters and I respected our parents immensely and always knew where the boundaries were set. We were made aware that if we went beyond those boundaries then consequences would follow. However, for most of the time we did not push those limits too far.

When I reflect on my childhood I am so glad we were part of a large and close-knit family with plenty of aunts, uncles, cousins and grandparents, all of whom lived fairly nearby. My sisters and I often dropped in to see our grandparents on the way home from school, besides visiting with them on Sunday evenings after church. We also had many friends who lived on the same road. With these friends we sometimes wandered on the beach, enjoyed the local playground or went for walks along the Kilkeel Esplanade and around the harbour. I still look back on those days and am grateful that we had such an idyllic childhood.

In keeping up with our tomboyish life style we each had our favourite football team and enjoyed nothing better than watching "Match of the Day" on television with Dad every Saturday night and routing for our rival teams. We also had great fun and at times, a few fights, in kicking a ball around the field at the back of our home. Sports became a big part of my life and I became involved in the athletics and hockey programme at school.

Most summers were spent on the local beach dipping in and out of the tide with our friends. It never occurred to us that we were missing out on anything. As we got older, it did not bother us in the least that we were not allowed to do what our peers were doing or go where they went. We were perfectly happy with our lives.

Of course, because we were born into a Christian home, church played a major part in our lives. We attended Kilkeel Baptist Tabernacle and the Sunday School there every week. I cannot ever remember a time when I did not want to go to church. However, although our parents taught us right from wrong and I always tried to please them and do the very best I could, yet I knew that I needed to be saved. I really did not have any desire to become involved in the so-called "things of the world", but I still knew that I was a sinner in need of salvation. From as far back as I can remember I knew that Christ died on the cross for me and I needed to come to Him for pardon and eternal life. However, like many young people, I thought I had plenty of time and that I could put it off until I was older. I was planning to live for a very long time and the thought of death never crossed my mind.

In 1971 some workers from Child Evangelism Fellowship conducted a Five-day Bible Club in our town and my two sisters and I attended every day. I cannot remember much of what was said during the course of that week, but two verses spoke to me then and have stayed with me ever since. The first was in Matthew 25:13; "Watch therefore for ye know neither the day nor the hour in which the Son of Man cometh." The other verse was 2 Corinthians 6:2; "Behold now is the accepted time, behold now is the day of salvation." I already knew that I was not prepared for eternity and that the Lord could return at any time. However, it was at those meetings that I fully realised that if Jesus was to come that day, I would not have been ready. When the meeting finished I waited behind and sitting on a grass verge in the open air, I put my trust in Jesus Christ, asked Him to forgive my sin and save me.

As I was only ten years old, there was not a dramatic change in my life. However, the Lord did take control of my rather hot temper. I had always felt exonerated from blame for my temper tantrums for I felt they were well-matched with my red hair. Nevertheless, the Lord came into my life and not only gave me a real peace and assurance of knowing Him, but forgiveness and cleansing too for my hot temper. Since those childhood days I have proved God's power to keep and have been aware of His presence in my life.

In 1975 Mum and Dad made major decisions that would affect our lives and bring big changes to our home. One evening Mum and Dad sat us three girls down and told us how the Lord had been leading them into New Tribes Mission. This meant that we would have to move to the United States to be with our parents while they did their missionary training. Even though Mum and Dad had kept us informed all along, I never actually thought they would really go through with their plans. That is why it came as a real shock to my system when they finally announced that we were leaving.

I was in third form at Kilkeel High School at that time and loved it. The thought of saying goodbye to my friends and family, plus having to leave all the things with which I felt comfortable and secure, really petrified me. Added to this was the fear and uncertainty of what might lie ahead for us. It was during that traumatic time that I was able to prove the Lord in my own life. Prior to this I had been drifting along in my Christian life and had not really grown much. I had neglected to see the importance of spending time alone with God in prayer. However, as the date for departure drew closer, I began to realise that although I was leaving all my friends and family, yet I had a Friend who would never leave me, nor would He ever disappoint or fail me. Although I had neglected Him in earlier days, yet I had the assurance that I was in God's safekeeping no matter where I lived. Through those days I discovered that trusting in God's faithfulness could dispel my fearfulness.

We did not find it easy to adapt to the different culture at the New Tribes Training centre. Our problems and difficulties seemed to build up and become insurmountable. Wilma, Eunice and I had to make new friends, even though we stuck closely to each other. It was not easy to fit into a completely different educational system. It also meant our attending three different schools during the two years we were in the USA when we moved from Wisconsin to Michigan and finally to Missouri. Our time in America was not only training ground for Mum and Dad, we all had to learn to cast all our care on the Lord Jesus and prove that He truly cared for us.

We, the three McConnell sisters, were quite a novelty when we started school in the United States. Because we hailed from Ireland some people thought our first language was Irish. They were therefore very impressed with our command of the English language even though they found our accent hard to understand. We had to slow down our speech for their benefit.

Their education system was as much a mystery to us as ours was to them. Unlike our seven years of High School, they had only four years so they had no idea where to slot us in.

We thought the French class was brilliant when we discovered that we didn't actually have to learn any French. In our American school they studied French culture and French food and we even prepared and had to eat a French meal at our teacher's home. Occasionally we had to read some French, but we never had to do any translating. As for French grammar, Wilma seemed to know more than the teacher and a number of times he even asked for her opinion.

In our science class we discussed evolution and the origin of the species.

Wilma and I, along with an American lad, were the only ones to disagree with the teacher. He subsequently arranged a class where we were allowed to present our views on creation. We gathered up some material, which we were able to put on display as we presented the Biblical case for creation. Two teachers and other students listened and then debated with us. As a result of that opportunity quite a few students began to consider for the first time that creation was a plausible approach. We really felt the Lord had given us wisdom and strength for that day.

Eunice and I enjoyed our Drivers' Education class, which we were able to take when we were fifteen years old. At that young age they even let us loose behind the wheel on the highway. Since the car had automatic transmission it was easier for us to drive. Nevertheless, we did prove to be quite a challenge to the instructor when we kept venturing to the opposite side of the road.

Unfortunately for us, neither hockey nor football were on the curriculum, but I did find volleyball a good substitute However, I never found the same enthusiasm for baseball, basketball or American football, although we did participate.

In the 1970s the world wasn't as small as it is now. Back then there was a lot less international travel and therefore, less understanding of cultural differences. We found some aspects of American culture difficult to understand and it took time for us to get used to the American English. When we were offered "Kool-Aid" we didn't know whether to accept or refuse it. If "tea" was included on a menu we had to decipher between "hot tea" and "ice tea". Their "sidewalk" was our "footpath" and we discovered that a "restroom" was not a place to relax. It was a toilet. Their "candy" did not taste nearly as good as our "sweets" and we could not understand why anyone would want to eat "supper" at 6.00pm.

There were lots of fun times when we enjoyed games of volleyball and I recall one occasion when the boys challenged the girls to a game of soccer. They assured everyone they would thrash us hands down, but it was obvious that they were not aware of our tomboyish history. We carefully worked out our tactics and had them running all over the field. The boys finally gave up when the score reached 10 – 0 in our favour.

Needless to say, after that the McConnell girls were never left on the sidelines when it came to choosing teams for soccer.

We made good friends with many of the single missionary students and the other missionaries' kids. We met with them for times of fellowship and Bible study and enjoyed opportunities to go witnessing with them in one of the local towns. At that time I found it nerve-wrecking and frightening to witness to strangers, but in retrospect the experience really did help us to rely on the Lord and to study God's Word. It was then that I learned the words of 1 Peter 3:15; "But sanctify the Lord God in your hearts, and be ready always to give an answer to every man that asketh you a reason of the hope that is in you, with meekness and fear."

After Mum and Dad completed their time in the United States in 1977 we returned home to Kilkeel. It was good for us to be back among our family and friends again and to catch up on all that we had missed during our two years' absence from Northern Ireland.

After another two years we moved again, this time to the New Tribes Bible School in Matlock, Derbyshire, where Mum and Dad were invited to help on the staff. While in England I got a job in a supermarket in Matlock. I enjoyed the job very much and was able to work my way up to the position of assistant manager.

1980 brought more major changes to our home when both Wilma and Eunice decided to get married. Wilma married Malcolm whom she had met at the church we attended in Derbyshire. Eunice married Norman whom she had dated before we moved to England. The departure of my two sisters from our home in the same year meant I was left alone and I missed them terribly even though they did not move too far away from us, that is, until Norman and Eunice moved back to Northern Ireland in 1983.

Living at New Tribes Bible School brought us into contact with the dedicated staff and many of the students as they prepared for various mission fields. Being on campus meant I was able to become part of the student life and enjoy many competitive games. It also meant being dragged out of bed to join them on early morning jogs and I had opportunity to sit in on a few of the evening lectures. Those days made a great impression on my own spiritual life.

During the years away from the "Kingdom of Mourne" I was able to keep in touch with many of my friends at my home church. I returned to Kilkeel each year to attend our church's youth weekends. After four years of being at "home alone" in Matlock, late in 1984 I finally moved back to Northern Ireland to live with my Nana McConnell in Kilkeel. I was able to obtain a transfer from my job in Matlock to Wellworths in Newry as both were owned by the same company.

It was just after going back to live in Kilkeel that I met Andrew Shields. A few years earlier his family had moved to Sandilands Caravan Park in Cranfield, near Kilkeel. In contrast to me, Andrew was born in the "big smoke", as some would call Belfast, on December 20th 1962. He and his older brother, William, grew up on a farm near Ballynahinch, which is also in County Down.

William was more involved in the farm whereas Andrew only got involved when help was really necessary. Andrew took more interest in motor bikes and began to ride them when he was only thirteen years old. This obviously accounted why Craig and Scott would later take to motocross at the same age; it was definitely in the Shields' blood.

During his school holidays Andrew loved nothing better than accompanying his father on his many trips around Ireland. Mr. Shields worked in sales and clocked up many miles each year covering both Northern Ireland and the Irish Republic. This is where Andrew probably gained his good sense of direction whereas I can easily become lost in a shopping centre.

The Shields family attended Carr Baptist Church and the two boys became involved with the youth group in their church and the nearby Boardmills Presbyterian Church. Wesley McCullough was the leader of the Boys' Brigade Bible Class at Boardmills Presbyterian Church. Andrew, who was enrolled in the BB company, attended the Bible Class every Sunday. Wesley made a big impression on Andrew's young heart and through Wesley, God spoke to Andrew many times about his need of salvation, but without much response. Finally, after an evangelistic mission at Carr Baptist Church in 1979, Andrew repented from his sin and put his trust in Jesus Christ as personal Saviour.

In June 1982 Mr & Mrs Shields moved from Ballynahinch to Kilkeel with their two boys to become the proprietors of Sandilands Caravan Park at Cranfield, which is only a few miles along the coast from Kilkeel. Like us moving to the United States, initially, Andrew was not altogether happy about this move. Besides having to leave his friends in Ballynahinch, he also had a long distance to travel to work in Belfast where he was employed in the Gents' Outfitting Department of Millar Boyd and Reid. It was the young people at Kilkeel Baptist Tabernacle who helped Andrew eventually settle into a new way of life in Kilkeel.

I am not only glad that Andrew came from Ballynahinch at that time, but I returned from England two years later. It was obviously meant to be. After accepting the offer of a lift home from Andrew one Sunday evening after the Young People's Fellowship our friendship developed and soon we started dating. In the subsequent months we gradually got to know each other and discovered that we had similar interests. My knowledge of soccer and the fact that I was not a Manchester United supporter proved to be a great asset, especially as Andrew later qualified to be a football referee. I must confess I had to be educated on the rules of motocross.

Within a short time we realised that the Lord had brought us together. We became engaged to be married on 7th March 1986 and were married in Kilkeel Baptist Tabernacle exactly one year later, the day after the terrible Zeebrugge Ferry disaster when one hundred and eighty-seven people lost their lives.

Andrew and I were young, we were in love and just starting out on life together. In spite of the wet and windy weather it did not dampen our excitement and joy on our special day.

"Life offers us choices. Christ graciously offers us forgiveness for what is past, peace for the present and wisdom for what lies ahead" (Alison's Journal).

3

Our Happy Family

After Andrew and I returned from our honeymoon in Gran Canaria we moved in with Andrew's parents at their home in Sandilands Caravan Park. We remained there until we built our own house adjacent to theirs in 1990.

After our first son, Craig, was born in May 1988, we decided that I should have a career break, at least until all our children would be attending school. This turned out to be a longer career break than we could ever have imagined.

Our second son, Scott, was born in October of the following year. We found it was very convenient having Andrew's parents on hand to help out as my parents were serving the Lord in Papua New Guinea with New Tribes Mission. They did not return until late 1993. Our little family remained in Andrew's parents' home until our own home was completed in December 1990.

Our third child, Kyle Thomas William, who was called for both his grandfathers, was born on 18th October 1992. He weighed in at 8lbs 14oz. and was declared to be a healthy, normal, bouncing baby boy.

To be truthful, I had been secretly hoping for a baby girl after already having two boys. I remember being slightly disappointed when the midwife announced, "It's another boy." However, that disappointment only lasted a few seconds until a little bundle that was my precious little baby was placed in my arms. I fell in love with him immediately and was just so thankful that we had another healthy son, or at least, so we thought.

We all suffered a sudden and severe blow when Andrew's father passed away suddenly just a few months after Kyle was born in January 1993. We are so grateful that Grandad Shields, who was affectionately known to the grandchildren as 'Nanda', got to meet and know Kyle before he went home to heaven.

As a baby Kyle was never a great sleeper. He was always extremely restless and I cannot remember ever getting a whole night's sleep. He seemed to be prone to chest and kidney infections and during his first year he received ten courses of antibiotics. I never seemed to be out of the doctor's surgery, but this did not unduly perturb me as little Kyle met all the initial developmental stages for infants; he was sitting up, crawling and walking. Having raised two other boys who were remarkably healthy, I initially thought Kyle must be a sickly baby and that as he got older he would eventually grow out of these infections.

Kyle's first visit to a hospital was in September 1993 when he was only eleven months old. He needed an intravenous antibiotic for a prolonged kidney infection. This would be the first of countless hospital appointments over the next thirteen years. On this initial visit to the hospital Kyle turned out to be every doctor's worst nightmare. It was practically impossible to find a vein to inject. The only place they could find a suitable vein was on the side of his head. This was a painful procedure for Andrew and me to watch. Kyle was our darling baby boy and it hurt us to see a needle go into his wee head. However, the doctors assured us that it sounded a lot worse than it actually was and that the screaming was because Kyle had to be restrained during the procedure.

Over the next weeks Kyle was subjected to further investigations and scans to try to discover why he was having these repeated infections. As a result it was concluded that Kyle had a reflux to his right kidney. He eventually had an operation for this in the Ulster Hospital when he was only eighteen months old. This operation prevented further kidney infections. However, Kyle also had constant nasal problems and so, just nine months later in December 1995, he underwent more surgery to have his adenoids removed at Newry's Daisy Hill Hospital.

It was probably about this time I began to realise that there was something different about Kyle. When he was almost three years old I noticed his development was much slower than what his older brothers had been. Initially this only gave us mild concern. I was consoled by other parents who said they had children who were slow to walk or to talk. Having listened to these other mothers I felt reassured that everything would be all right and that Kyle would soon catch up with other boys in his age group. However, the opposite seemed to be happening.

As he became older it was evident that Kyle was also developing severe behavioural problems. His speech was limited, potty training was turning out to be a complete disaster and he was still wakening many times in the night. I recall many nights getting into bed beside him to try to settle him for maybe the fourth or fifth time within a few hours. This pattern went on for months and as a result I felt totally exhausted. In my distress I cried out to God and asked Him that someone somewhere may be able to find out what was wrong with our darling little Kyle. Andrew and I felt that if we only knew what Kyle's problem was then we would try to get him whatever treatment or medication was necessary. After that we could return to resuming a normal life and maybe be able to enjoy an uninterrupted nights' sleep.

We were able to enrol Kyle in a local playgroup in September 1995. He was supposed to be potty trained before he started and I vividly remember setting him on the potty before leaving home. I tried to encourage him in every way I could and even ran the water taps in a forlorn hope that he might perform. It pleased me immensely when he obliged. The fact that the playgroup only lasted for a few hours meant that Kyle was usually fine until he arrived home. I then put his "pull-ups" back on and we returned to what was normality for us.

The carers at the playgroup found Kyle to be such a handful that they had to assign one of the helpers to look after him. Kyle was so hyperactive that he always had to be on the move and appeared unable to concentrate on any activity for more than a few seconds. His playtimes never seemed to include anything constructive. Kyle was always more intent on destruction. Even when we tried to restrain him he merely shook us off and carried on regardless. Despite correcting him frequently he appeared to have no conception of what the word 'no' actually meant. Even if we did feel he had finally understood what it meant, it was all forgotten by the following day. We loved Kyle to bits, but it was most frustrating to see that his behaviour pattern was so different from anything we had experienced with his two brothers, Craig and Scott.

Another year passed and Kyle was due to commence nursery school in September 1996. As with all new starters, it was planned that I should take Kyle into the school for a short stay before the school year finished at the end of the June term. This was to help familiarise the children with the school and let them meet the staff. Kyle was in his element when he got there! There was so much for him to see and do, but nothing seemed to sustain his interest for any length of time. He ran from one table to another; he swiped at puzzles, lifted pencils, grabbed books and chewed on the crayons. During all this dreadful behaviour I was running after him trying to restrain him and repair the damage he had left in his wake.

The school sandpit seemed to be familiar territory for Kyle. He had already acquired a taste for sand from our many trips to Cranfield Beach, which was only a hundred yards from our home. When I found him in the sandpit he was having a right royal feast and it took some effort to drag him away. I was totally exhausted from trying to keep up with Kyle to prevent too much damage.

During all this bizarre behaviour from our son I was keenly aware that all the other parents were watching him and me. At times I felt crushed for I could hear them talking among themselves. As far as they were concerned, Kyle was an unruly brat who was spoilt rotten and all he needed was a bit of good old-fashioned discipline at home.

Perhaps not surprisingly, by the end of the hour when there would be a review of the session at the playschool, the school principal informed me that it would be impossible for them to cope with Kyle. Therefore, they would definitely not be offering him a place in the next school term. I had been extremely embarrassed by the way other parents had looked and spoken about us, but was now totally shattered that the principal had refused to offer a place for Kyle at the nursery school for the following term. I never even had considered this as a possibility. Until then I had never heard of a child being refused a placement under these circumstances. The whole experience had left me completely drained and I returned home in tears.

In retrospect, and with the knowledge that I later acquired, I realize I should have fought for my child and should have been more determined in trying to find answers to why Kyle was behaving as he did. It was only with the process of time that I learned to be assertive when it came to sorting things for him. I was neither authoritative nor aggressive by nature and I found it very difficult to adopt such an attitude. I tried to do anything and everything just to make things better for Kyle. I was always trying to accommodate him into a normal situation when I really should have been pushing for Kyle to have a special needs placement with a classroom assistant, on a one to one basis. However, at that time I did not even know what a "special needs placement" was. All I knew was that I had a son whom I loved greatly and tried to educate in proper social behaviour, but whom I could not control. I had given the same attention and instruction to his older brothers, Craig and Scott, and they had responded positively. After all, they had also benefited from the same playschool from which Kyle had been rejected.

All this prompted more questions in our minds about Kyle, but I still did not know why he was behaving in this manner. There was no one to turn to or anyone who could tell me why this was happening to our little boy whom Andrew and I loved so much. We wanted Kyle to grow up to enjoy life and be accepted by his peers, but things were looking ominous.

By this time Kyle was having tests for his delayed physical development, but we still had received no answers. I just felt I was at the end of my tether.

After the trauma of the visit to the playschool that morning, I was stunned and excited to receive a phone call that afternoon to tell me that I had won a holiday to Florida. I had entered a magazine competition without any expectation of winning, but this was a welcome break. When I reflect on the timing of it all I can only conclude that it must have been God's way of taking my mind of what had happened earlier in the day. I do remember it did make me feel much better.

The holiday was brilliant and we all got a much-needed break.

"Life is a journey in which Jesus Christ wants to be our constant Companion" (Alison's Journal).

4

Trying To Find Answers

When Kyle was three and a half years old at the end of April 1996, he was referred to the child development team at Craigavon Area Hospital for tests. Originally the doctor had attributed Kyle's delayed development to his having had major surgery for his kidney reflux while still an infant. However, it was also thought that by three years old he would have caught up.

Kyle was examined by the doctors on the development programme and a number of medical tests were carried out. For these to be completed a urine sample was needed, but Kyle would not perform at that time. As a result, I suggested taking a sample of his urine to our local hospital the following week to be sent off for testing. This was readily agreed upon and I took the sample to Newry as planned and gave it to the nurse for testing. The nurse did a routine test for infection and then discarded the rest of the sample, not realising that it was also supposed to go for genetic testing. I'm sure the nurse was not very popular for her actions.

When the nurse told me about her mistake I knew there was no way we were going to easily obtain another sample at the hospital. I was sent home, therefore, with another sample bottle to be taken to our local clinic. The label on the sample bottle read, "Test for Mucopolysaccharide Disease". This was the first time I had ever seen this word *mucopolysaccharide* and I did not even know how to pronounce it, much less what it meant.

I think most people would have reacted as I did. My curiosity made me determined to try to find out what *mucopolysaccharide disease* meant and what they were actually testing Kyle for. First, I got the dictionary out and looked up the definition which said: *Any of the polysaccharides that form chemical bonds with water to produce mucilaginous and lubricating fluids and which contain sugar derivatives such as amino acids.* I was none the wiser and did not have a clue what all that meant.

Andrew had a doctor's appointment for the following week so I persuaded him to ask about this *mucopolysaccharide disease* while he was there. Our GP told Andrew that it was an extremely rare genetic disorder, but that we should try not to worry about it at present. Although he did not know of any cases he promised to find some information for us.

One of my hobbies is doing competitions and I have won several prizes over the years, including the previously mentioned holiday to Florida. Due to this interest I bought the *Chat* and *Take A Break* magazines most weeks just to do the puzzles. Very rarely did I ever have time to read any of the articles in the magazines. Kyle ensured that I was always too busy. However, towards the end of May that year, just a month after going to the hospital for the urine tests, I was flicking through the *Take A Break* magazine when my eyes were drawn to a particular story. The word "mucopolysaccharide" seemed to jump out of the page at me. I realised that here was that word again. I started to read avidly.

The magazine story was about two little boys who had this disorder. At the time it did not register with me who these boys were or to what family they belonged. However, as I read through the article which told of their behavioural problems, their sleeplessness, their hyperactivity and how they had physically developed to a certain point and then began to regress, I quickly recognised that all the symptoms were very similar to Kyle's. By now I was totally engrossed in the article and read on about the syndrome. The report disclosed that the condition was terminal and there was no known cure.

I knew that the Bible tells us not to worry, but my practice of "casting all my care upon Him" did not seem to be working. I seemed to have so many questions without any answers. My mind was in a whirl racing from one question to another. *Was this what Kyle had?* It certainly ticked all the right boxes. *Was his condition terminal? What would it mean to us as a family? How could we cope? It could not possibly be this, or could it? I knew that God really loved us, but how could He possibly allow something as painful as this to happen in our lives? Would God allow Kyle to be taken from us?* I tried not to worry, but try as I would, I kept falling into the anxiety trap.

Although Kyle's urine sample had been sent in April it was October before we finally got the results. Meanwhile, Kyle had to undergo further blood tests and these were sent to London for analysis. Nothing happened too quickly and life seemed to be spent endlessly hanging around hospital waiting rooms and having consultations with various doctors and consultants. During this time I was trying to make home life as normal as possible for Craig and Scott while coping with little Kyle who seemed to have boundless stores of energy and was becoming quite unstoppable.

There were occasions during those long months when I was able to put all the anxiety to the back of my mind, but at other times I found myself watching Kyle, remembering what I had read about those two little boys and looking for any similarities in him. I also recall one evening, just a few days before we were due to receive Kyle's results, that I was at a Mum and Toddlers meeting when a friend asked me if I thought Kyle really did have this disease with the big long name. Even though I told her "No", I knew I was really only trying to convince myself and perhaps cushion myself from reality. I was obviously in denial. Ever since I had read the magazine article I also recognised and harboured the thought at the back of my mind that this was the same as what Kyle had.

In my more rational moments I knew that nothing ever happens by chance or accident. I believed that God was in control of everything and I now acknowledge that reading the magazine article was God's way of preparing us for the news that we were soon to receive. Yes, this was God's doing, but it would not make it any easier when news confirming our worst fears came as a tremendous shock.

"Is it because of my ignorance and weak faith that I often think something to be against me when in reality it is for me and working for my good?" (Alison's Journal)?

5

The Results Are In

I still clearly recall the last day of October 1996. That Thursday will remain in our memories for the rest of our lives. Originally we were due to receive the results of Kyle's tests early in November, but because the clinics were closed for Halloween, Dr Magee from the genetics team, phoned to enquire if it would be convenient for us to meet her on that day.

Conversation between Andrew and me was limited as we travelled to Craigavon for the appointment. We were still hoping against hope that Kyle might have some illness or syndrome that was treatable and not this incomprehensible devastating disease with its unpronounceable name.

A speech therapist took Kyle to play while Dr Magee and Dr Bell took Andrew and me into a private room at the child development clinic. The atmosphere in the room was surreal. I wanted the time to rush by quickly because I could not wait to hear what was the matter with Kyle.

At the same time I wanted time to stand still for I had a dreadful foreboding that we were now going to hear a result that we were not prepared to accept.

I listened as the doctors spoke, but my attention was almost impassive. Although both doctors were measured in their speech it seemed to us that our son's life was torn apart by their clinical words and phrases. The doctors informed us that Kyle did have a *mucopolysaccharide* disease (MPS) which was known as *Sanfilippo*. This diagnosis only confirmed our worst fears, but it also showed that the Lord had already been preparing us for this traumatic hour. Both doctors further explained all about the disease, how that it was an extremely rare genetic condition which only affected one in every 85,000 births in the United Kingdom. They also told us that the syndrome was terminal. There was no known cure for *Sanfilippo* and that Kyle would probably have a life expectancy of about fourteen years.

Both doctors were very sympathetic, but at the same time they were frank and honest. Andrew and I were in a state of shock and were not able to take in very much of the details and medical information the doctors were giving us. In addition to all the verbal information, we were also given leaflets and contact names. It was further agreed that we should return to the hospital for another appointment a week later. This appointment was undoubtedly arranged because by then we would be more prepared to talk about the diagnosis and the doctors would be available to answer any questions we might have. That intervening week dragged by and was one of the longest weeks of our lives.

We left the room that Thursday morning in a daze. We were unable to understand or fully comprehend what we had just been told. I managed to keep myself under control and fought back my mixed-up emotions, until I met Kyle. He came flying down the corridor with the speech therapist hurrying after him. He was his usual happy, boisterous self and greeted us with a wide smile and giggle, but I just went to pieces. It suddenly hit me that my wee man had a disease that would eventually kill him and we would never see him grow up. What was worse was that there was absolutely nothing that we could do about it.

I'm not sure how we made our way back home from Craigavon to Kilkeel. Tears streamed down our faces during the whole journey. It is impossible to put into words just how we felt. We were utterly devastated. It seemed as though our whole world had fallen apart that day. It was just so hard to absorb that our extremely active and rambunctious four-year-old boy was so seriously ill and would have such a brief life.

We all have dreams and aspirations for our children. Every boy has the potential to grow up and become a famous footballer, a rugby star, a teacher or a doctor. The possibility of having a disabled son in a wheelchair never entered into the equation. I had never planned for this or even contemplated the likelihood of anything like this happening.

I was in an emotional turmoil. The inner pain was excruciating, especially when I thought of all the changes that would eventually take place in Kyle's brief life, both physically and mentally. I did not want him to look different from other children; I did not want people staring at him or whispering about his condition. Like any parent, I wanted our son to grow up normal and not have to face the progressive decline that this disease would inevitably bring.

Even though we tried to protect Craig and Scott from the trauma that Andrew and I were experiencing, yet they sensed something was wrong. Craig was eight and a half years old and Scott was seven. After some discussion Andrew and I decided it was only right that we should be as open and honest with them as the medical staff had been with us. We were also afraid that if we did not tell them, they might find out about Kyle's illness from other children at school or even overhear something from our conversations on the phone.

When we told the boys they listened in as much silence as Andrew and I had done at the hospital and were just as non-plussed as we had been. We answered their questions honestly and openly letting them know all that we knew, but at a level that we felt they would understand. It was hard to explain that Kyle would die some day, but, at the same time, we hoped to still have him for a good few years, if God allowed it. Although there were tears initially the two brothers soon realised that even though they knew Kyle was ill, yet he would still be Kyle. He had not changed and he was still the same destructive yet loveable, wee brother that he had always been.

During those initial days following Kyle's diagnosis our home resembled an Irish funeral wake. We were inundated with kind people calling to offer their condolences. Dozens of cards and letters of support arrived by post. We were very grateful for all these visits, tokens of support and offers of help for, in a way, we were grieving deeply as if it was a family death. In reality, we were broken-hearted at all that Kyle was losing. We felt he had been robbed of his health and cheated of a normal life with any future opportunities. We lamented at all the things he would not be able to do.

Of course, this was not a funeral wake. Kyle was not only present, he proved to be very much alive and kept everyone entertained with his lively antics. Visitors even had to learn to be on their guard as Kyle was responsible for spilling many cups of tea or coffee on them during their visits. Kyle's presence made the whole situation somewhat bizarre for while the people came to sympathise with us about Kyle, our energetic boy not only dominated their conversation, he was often the centre of their attention.

At this time Andrew's Mum was in Australia visiting her brother and sister and their families. We very much wanted to tell her about Kyle's diagnosis and the prognosis, however we did not want to spoil her holiday. We knew her thoughts would constantly be drifting back to us in Ireland and wondering how we might be coping with the whole situation.

After a long-distance telephone call with his uncle about our dilemma, Andrew and his uncle made a joint decision not to tell Bertha anything about the matter until she returned home in December. Bertha already knew that Kyle was having investigations, but was unaware of when the results might be expected. It would be better for her to enjoy her holiday and relax before returning to our stressful circumstances at home. She would need all the strength gained from her trip for the ensuing months.

During these times I had to ask myself if all this could really be happening. I felt as if someone was going to tell us the whole thing was a weird mistake and that Kyle was fine. At the same time, I had known in my heart for some time that there was something wrong with my wee man. Andrew and I had even prayed for answers to the dilemma, but to hear from the doctors that he had this MPS disease sent my head spinning with all sorts of thoughts. *How would it all be when Kyle would not be around to tuck him up into bed at night or to keep me awake in the wee hours of the morning? How would I cope as his disease progressed? How will I ever say goodbye to our little boy? How could we ever be prepared to lose our wee son whom we loved so dearly?*

After some time the sympathy cards stopped coming, the phone eventually went silent and the steady stream of visitors finally dried up. Even though I knew that people had to get on with their own lives, I began to have unkind and resentful thoughts towards people who were my good friends. At times I became resentful and I felt that no one cared any more. Perhaps it was because I appeared to be so calm and positive on the outside and developed such a tough exterior that people failed to see the hurt and pain I was feeling beneath the surface. After all, this was my son who was dying and I had no control over it at all.

Generally, we grow up expecting to lose our grandparents and maybe, even our parents in some distant day, but not our children. This was the boy I gave birth to, the little bundle we held in our arms and loved unreservedly. To us the whole situation just did not make sense or have any meaning. As parents we look forward to being there for our children through every stage of their lives, from starting school through to their teenage years and into adulthood. We want to share in the joy of seeing them graduate, meet a girl, attend their wedding and enjoy grandchildren. None of these things would happen to Kyle. The bottom had fallen out of all our hopes and expectations.

Stupid things began to enter my mind. For example, I felt it would be pointless keeping Scott's football boots as hand-me-downs for Kyle, for he would never need them. Neither was there any sense in keeping Scott's school uniform for Kyle or his books from school. Little things like this became totally overwhelming at times. At other times I found myself watching other children around Kyle's age and comparing their abilities to his. It was devastating for us to realise that with Kyle we would never witness the developments that other parents took for granted. We had no choice but to watch our son suffer this progressive deterioration which would eventually result in a premature death.

It was during these times that I was tempted to question God's handling of our situation. At the same time I had to remind myself that God is to be trusted at all times for His way is always perfect; "As for God, His way is perfect, the Word of the Lord is proved He is a shield to all those who trust in Him" (Psalm 18v30).

What do you do when your whole world has been turned upside down? Through this painful experience I have learned that the only true security in life comes from placing our trust in the God who created us, the One who loves us and Who is in complete control of our lives. Without His strength and the support of so many family and friends, I do not know how we would have made it through. We are forever grateful to our closest friends and our families. We thank God for our former Pastor, Geoffrey Ward, and our present Pastor, Alan Dundas, who gave us unstinting prayerful and practical support through those trying years. Their pastoral support, care and love helped make many of our burdens more bearable. Our friends also helped us carry our weighty burdens when we were incredibly weak, they wept with us when we shed our tears and prayed with us when we were so low.

Through all the spiritual numbness, mental confusion and emotional roller-coaster that we were experiencing, there was also a keen awareness that in spite of all the unknown factors and formidable fears, God was with us and had put His peace in our hearts. I was reminded what God told Moses in Exodus 33:14; "My presence shall go with thee, and I will give thee rest." I had to cling to this promise and hold on to the truth that God was in absolute control and His will is always best, even when it did not line up with mine.

I tried to maintain a personal quiet time with the Lord even though it was difficult at times during those hectic days. Often this was incorporated into many of my nightly visits to be with Kyle. I remember on one such occasion reading Jeremiah 29:11; "I know the plans I have for you, plans to prosper you and not to harm you, plans to give you a hope and a future." To me this meant that God had a plan for Kyle and even if I did not fully understand, He would work it all out. I was going to have to walk by faith through these days and depend fully on my God.

Romans 8;28 also gave me quite a measure of reassurance; "And we know that all things work together for good to them that love God, to them who are called according to his purpose..." This meant that God would always do what was best for us. I would just have to trust Him each day for the necessary strength to survive and remember He was in control.

I have discovered that it was easy to repeat and believe verses when things were going well, but when events fail to turn out as we had hoped and planned, that is when our faith is tested. I had heard it said that the faith that is not tested cannot be trusted.

I also recognised that the Lord had heard my prayers for healing for Kyle, but the Lord in His wisdom had this time answered "No." With the passing of time my prayers for healing, gradually became prayers for strengthening until I was able to say with the Psalmist, "Blessed be the Lord, because he hath heard the voice of my supplication. The Lord is my strength and my shield; my heart trusted in Him, and I am helped; therefore my heart greatly rejoiceth; and with my song will I praise Him. The Lord is their strength, and He is the saving strength of His anointed" (Psalm 28:6-8).

My prayer time experiences were quite amazing. Prayer did not always bring the things that I desired or even change my circumstances. Through prayer God gave us the strength we needed to bear the burden He had placed upon us and provided us with the peace and calm needed to be able to accept the situation. I had to marvel at the change God gradually brought in my attitude. He really does give us "songs in the night" of our experience and peace in the midst of the tempestuous storms of our lives.

Andrew and I discovered there was life after this dreaded *Sanfilippo disease*. We had two other boys to rear. Andrew had to continue his work. I had to carry on with the routine of housekeeping, cooking meals and attending to the needs of my husband and sons. We kept our involvement with the work at Kilkeel Baptist Tabernacle and tried to maintain some sort of social contact with our friends. We continued pursuing our daily lives, not as we had planned, but according to His plan.

"Our afflictions are not designed to break us, but to bring us to God" (Alison's Journal).

6

Our Special Child

Just after Kyle's diagnosis, a friend of Andrew's Mum gave me a tape recording of Phyllis Arnold's testimony. Phyllis and her husband, Hartford, had two sons who were born with a congenital syndrome and after several years both boys died within a short time of each other. I remember listening to the testimony as I drove into town. By the time I got to Kilkeel I was crying uncontrollably and had to return home.

Phyllis actually wrote a great book, *Some Party In Heaven* (Ambassador), in which she told of the trauma and testing of their painful experience. In the book Phyllis told of a nurse who gave her a poem just after she had given birth to her second handicapped son. It was that poem which really touched my heart:

HEAVEN'S VERY SPECIAL CHILD

A meeting was held quite far from earth,
'It's time again for another birth',
Said the angels to the Lord above.
This special child will need much love,
His progress may seem very slow.
Accomplishments he may not show,
And he'll require extra care
From the folk he meets down there.

He may not run or laugh or play,
His thoughts may seem quite far away.
In many ways he won't adapt,
And he'll be known as handicapped.
So let's be careful where he's sent,
We want his life to be content.
Please Lord find the parents who
Will do this special job for you.

They may not realise right away
This leading roll they're asked to play,
But with this child sent from above
Comes stronger faith and richer love,
And soon they'll know the privilege given
In caring for this child from Heaven,
Their precious child so meek, so mild
Is Heaven's very special child.

We read in the Bible how the Lord Jesus took the little children in His arms and blessed them. We must conclude that boys and girls were precious to Him; "And He took them up in His arms, put His hands upon them and blessed them." Jesus also said, 'Suffer the little children to come unto Me" (Mark 10:13-16).

We know that Kyle was a very special little boy to us and to God. We began to see that God had lent Kyle to us for a short season. We do not own any of our children. They are all gifts from God and given into our trust. At some stage we were going to have to give Kyle back to God who created him and loved him. For the present though, it was much easier to think about handling one day at a time and not to worry about the whole future at once. I was determined to enjoy the present moment. I found that in doing so I worried less about trivial things. When anxieties began to creep in I had to remind myself to keep casting my problems unto the Lord who exhorts, "Be therefore not anxious about tomorrow, for tomorrow will be anxious for the things of itself" (Matthew 6:34).

I also had to learn that when I prayed I had to hand my problems over to God and not take them back again to dwell on them. Hebrews 4:16 reminded me to "Approach the throne of grace with confidence so that I may receive mercy and find grace in my time of need."

I acknowledge that everybody reacts differently to the various trying situations in life. Each person also needs to learn to cope in their own particular way. I felt I needed to find out everything I could about this dreadful disease that had invaded our lives. I wanted to face the reality of what it meant and understand its details. I set about gleaning as much information as I could from our GP and from the worldwide web on my computer. I discovered there was a *Mucopolysaccharide* Society (MPS Society) for the benefit of those families affected by the disease.

Through this pursuit to find out more about the disease I learned that *Sanfilippo* is a *mucopolysaccharide disease* and is also known as *MPS III*. The disease takes its name from Dr Sanfilippo who was one of the doctors from the USA who first described the condition in 1963.

Mucopolysaccharides are long chains of sugar molecules used in the building of connective tissues in the body. *Saccharide* is a term for a sugar molecule and *poly* means many. *Muco* refers to the thick jelly-like consistency of the molecules.

In the normal body there is a continuous process of replacing used materials and breaking them down for disposal. Children with *Sanfilippo* syndrome are missing an enzyme that is essential in cutting up the used mucopolysaccharides. Therefore, these incompletely broken down mucopolysaccharides remain stored in cells in the body and cause progressive damage in the body instead of being disposed off as normal. Initially, infants and young children may show little sign of the disease, but as more and more cells become damaged the symptoms will eventually start to appear.

Sanfilippo disease is caused by a recessive gene. As Andrew, my husband, and I both carry this abnormal gene, there was a one in four chance with every pregnancy that our child would inherit the defective gene from each of us and therefore, would suffer from the disease. The doctors told us that the possibility of this happening was "like the throw of a dice," or as some would say, "luck". However, we knew there was more to it than that. For us, it was all in the providence of God. The Lord saw fit to bless us with two healthy boys, before we had Kyle.

We learned that Craig and Scott may also be carriers of this same recessive gene, but because the disease is so rare, the chances of them marrying another carrier are very slender. We know that God created Kyle, even with all his physical limitations due to this debilitating disease. God makes no mistakes. We knew Kyle's life, his future and his next breath were all in God's hand.

At present there is still no cure for Sanfilippo disease. Various methods have been used to try to replace the missing enzyme in the body, but none with any significant benefit. Bone marrow transplants have also been tried, but with disappointing results.

The disease tends to progress through three main stages. The first stage is generally manifested during pre-school years. In this stage the child will start to lag behind in his development and will begin to show signs of overactive and difficult behaviour. The diagnosis is seldom made very early as many of these children do not manifest any differences in their appearance. To complicate matters, some symptoms of *Sanfilippo* such as severe bouts of diarrhoea, frequent respiratory and ear infections, can also be common in a lot of normal children. Some families have had more than one affected child before any diagnosis had been established.

The second phase of *Sanfilippo* is characterised by extremely active, restless and very difficult behaviour. Most affected children sleep very little and will meddle in everything within their grasp. Sadly, speech and understanding will gradually be lost and some children never become potty trained. Even those who do, will eventually lose this trained routine.

In the third and final stages of the disease Sanfilippo children will slow down, lose their ability to walk, to feed themselves and will become totally dependent on nursing care.

I also learnt that children with Sanfilippo syndrome generally grow to a fairly normal stature. Their hair may be thicker and coarser and their bodies hairier than normal. Eyebrows are often dark and bushy and converge in the middle of the brow. The noses of Sanfilippo children tend to be upturned and flat at the bridge.

Life expectancy for the sufferers of Sanfilippo syndrome is extremely varied, but the average is around fourteen years. Some children do not even live that long while others have survived into their twenties.

All in all, humanly speaking, it is a rather bleak picture.

"True freedom is not in having our own way, but in yielding to God's way" (Alison's Journal).

7

Living With Sanfilippo

In many ways it was a relief when the doctors were able to diagnose, identify and put a name on Kyle's disease. It provided us with a valid reason for his severe behavioural problems. So often I had tried to discipline Kyle and encourage better behaviour. I had tried to teach him to talk, to be good, to be still, not to chew, not to throw things in the house or try to smash the television. All this was without any success.

I became aware that because of his limited understanding Kyle was not responsible for his actions nor would we be able to change him or his character. We would, therefore, have to adapt Kyle's surroundings to suit him. My worst nightmare was when we had to spend endless hours hanging around waiting rooms, whether it was at the dentist, the doctor or hospital clinics. Kyle always caused mayhem. At times I felt that in an ironical way he was trying to get his own back on the medical profession. He especially enjoyed meddling with the soil in the plant pots. If he was not trying to eat it he was tossing it out onto the floor.

He took great delight in throwing toys across the room regardless of who was in the firing line. At other times he just rolled about on the floor or belted down the corridor with me in hot pursuit.

'Hot' was undoubtedly the operative word during these escapades. I just got hotter and hotter under the collar when I noticed other parents whispering to each other about Kyle. Sometimes they rolled their eyes to the ceiling or just stared in disgust. As well as knowing what they were thinking, I now wanted to shout at them that Kyle was not a spoiled and undisciplined brat. The poor child just could not help his behaviour. Being the quiet and reserved person that I am, I remained tight-lipped and said nothing. It even got to the stage where we could not take Kyle out with us to visit people's houses. Having said that, our good friends who still received us in their homes knew to store away any valuable ornaments and remove everything that was not screwed down before Kyle arrived.

Thankfully, Kyle's GP, Dr Poots, was extremely understanding. He would always try to slot Kyle's appointments in between those of other patients. This meant we not only avoided having to wait around too long in the waiting room, but also spared his surgery from being attacked and demolished.

As Kyle's disease progressed, Dr Poots made himself available to be contacted at any time with any concerns we might have had. We appreciated his kindness for the many, many visits he paid to our home. The care and attention he gave to Kyle, and all of us, will always be remembered.

Likewise, Raymond Haugh, our dentist, often came back early from lunch to fit Kyle in first. In later years when Kyle was unable to manage going to the dental surgery, Raymond would visit and attend to Kyle regularly at our home, although any treatment that was needed had to be carried out under anaesthetic at hospital. It greatly helped to have such understanding professionals around us.

The MPS Society gave a lot of support and was able to offer a great deal of helpful advice. Discovering that many other children with Sanfilippo syndrome were not potty trained helped us enormously. I had tried potty-training Kyle from when he was two years old, but he had not really progressed. Kyle's idea of potty training was greatly at variance with mine. One minute he would be sitting on his potty and in the next he would be walking around with the potty on his head.

When I discovered that the child's inability to be potty trained was another feature of the Sanfilippo syndrome, I immediately gave up the idea of persisting in trying to train Kyle who was having severe bouts of diarrhoea. This was much easier contained in nappies and it took a great deal of pressure off me.

The MPS Society organised clinics and conferences in Northern Ireland. This enabled all the children with any of the MPS disorders to be seen by Dr Ed Wraith, a specialist in Mucopolysaccharide diseases. This spared the Northern Ireland patients having to travel to England to benefit from his expert advice. Dr Ed related very well to his patients and became well acquainted with their families. My husband, Andrew, maintained that Dr Ed might have had a good knowledge of the medical field, but he was not as knowledgeable when it came to the football field. Dr Ed was an ardent Newcastle United fan while our family were dyed in the wool Liverpool fanatics.

I remember the day I was asked by the MPS Society to give a talk at one of their Northern Ireland conferences. The very thought of standing up in front of over 100 people, many of them professionals, terrified me. However, for fifty nerve-racking minutes I spoke on "My son has Sanfilippo". The reasoning behind my participation at this conference was to enable the doctors and other professionals to gain an insight into the disease from a parent's perspective.

I had not only prepared thoroughly for this speech, but I had prayed earnestly and invited other friends to pray for me. The feedback afterwards was very encouraging. I was able to share a poem from Phyllis Arnold's testimony, "Heaven's Very Special Child". I also used the occasion to testify of how Andrew and I were relying on our Lord to strengthen and sustain us through the whole experience.

I was greatly surprised and pleased when the MPS Society asked if they could publish the text of my talk in their quarterly magazine. This publication is distributed to all the families throughout the United Kingdom who have loved ones affected with any of the MPS conditions.

We found that Kyle's hyperactivity was one of the most difficult things to cope with. He was totally reckless and had no sense of danger. However the MPS Society gave us very good practical advice about preparing a safe play area and making our home user-friendly for Kyle.

The dining room in our home at that time was just off the kitchen so we were able to adapt it to make a safe play area cum bedroom for Kyle. We had a split-door fitted so that when I was cooking or the boys were trying to do their homework, we could shut the bottom half of the door and still keep an eye on Kyle while he could also see us.

Padding was attached to the walls and floor and safety glass fitted in the window. The radiator was mounted high on the wall, as was also his television. In one corner of the room there was a ball pool which Kyle really enjoyed. A friend's daughter painted a mural of Postman Pat and Barney on the walls as part of her art project for school and this helped to brighten up his room.

Likewise, our kitchen had to be made "Kyle proof". Cupboards and drawers were fitted with childproof locks while all the work surfaces had to be kept clear. I reckon I must have had the tidiest kitchen in Ireland. After finding Kyle chewing on the lead of the electric kettle while it was still switched on, we had to quickly learn to disconnect it after use and not to leave it within Kyle's reach. On other occasions Kyle tried to turn on the gas hob or grab for a hot cup of tea totally unaware of the dangerous consequences.

Over the years Kyle hurled containers of household cleaners, bottles of cooking oil and cartons of milk or fruit juice. Many other items were shattered on the kitchen floor. Kyle has also been known to try and bounce eggs on the ceramic floor in the kitchen. He obviously thought the eggs were balls to play with. Needless to say, he soon discovered that eggs did not bounce like the other balls. However, this did not deter him from trying and trying again and again. As a result we had to have a chain fitted to the door of the refrigerator, much to the disappointment of our three cats and German Shepherd dog. They had thoroughly enjoyed cleaning up the mess.

Clearing up after Kyle became a regular chore. His antics were not too bad when contained in the kitchen, but I discovered that Sudocrem and talcum powder are not the easiest to remove from carpets.

Our microwave had to be encased because Kyle developed quite an obsession with switches and buttons. He would press the button on the microwave oven open the door and then slam it shut. He did not do this just once. The habit became a constant routine, press, open, slam, press, open, slam... Over and over again he followed an almost clockwork pattern. Kyle took the same delight in playing with the light switches. He seemed to be fascinated by the click of the switch and the light going on and off again. These switches had to be adjusted and were operated by keys, which were hung higher up the wall, likewise the kitchen television was mounted high on the wall, well out of reach from Kyle's tiny yet menacing fingers.

The main oven in the kitchen presented additional problems. Besides turning the gas on, Kyle loved opening the oven door and then banging it shut, that was when he was not trying to climb on top of the downward-opening door. He also loved to lift parts from off the gas rings. This resulted in removing all moveable parts and replacing them when I needed to use the oven and during the cooking time I had to ensure that Kyle was safely in his room.

Although Kyle ran around our home like a human tornado leaving a trail of destruction in his wake, it was never done in frustration or associated with anger, but with a gusto and exuberance for life. The articles that were either smashed on the ground or sent flying through the air were accompanied with joyful shouts of glee or childish giggles of laughter. Kyle was having great fun.

Any ornaments and valuables that had survived Kyle's early years were moved well out of his reach. All other doors out of the kitchen and living area had to be kept locked and the keys hung high beyond Kyle's reach. At times it felt as if we were living in a prison.

Kyle just did not know what to be up to next. For him everything had to be tried and tested. His every waking hour demanded our vigilant attention. Water taps were another one of his strange fascinations. Although we managed to avoid any major floods in our own home he did flood my Mum's bathroom.

Kyle loved to chew anything he could sink his teeth into. This included clothes, tea towels, and socks. It seemed as though anything and everything he got his hands on went straight into his mouth. Some of his favourite items included sand, soil, stones, flowers and paper. We have even had to retrieve coins from his mouth, nearly losing a finger in the process.

Rather than always safeguarding our property and belongings, we usually kept a supply of tea towels and soft items including baby teething rings for him to chew on. At least these were tastier than soggy socks or paper, furthermore, they posed less of a risk.

Although Kyle chewed on these unsavoury items, he also enjoyed his food. In the early years he could manage most foods as long as they were cut finely for him. He had his own large high chair and we let him feed himself while he was able, regardless of the mess he made. We did play some of his favourite TV programmes such as Barney, The Teletubbies or The Fimbles during meal times to try to distract him in the hope that he might eat the food instead of throwing it.

When drinking, Kyle used a baby's feeding cup with a non-spill lid. This was often turned upside down or thrown across the kitchen but it was less of a risk than with a normal cup. However, it did create problems when he began to chew on the cup lids. The damaged and distorted lids made it difficult for any juice to come through thereafter and they only lasted a short time. I decided to write to the manufacturers and explain the problems we were encountering with the cups. I had loads of cups, but all with non-useable lids. The company kindly replied and sent us a complimentary supply of lids.

When Kyle was three years old he could say a few words such as our names. Beyond that he was only able to string together sentences of three or four words. Most of these were associated with the family and included calling "Craig" or "Scott" "A bad boy", "Daddy's car" or "Grandma's house". "Ball" was definitely his favourite word. His little eyes would light up when he spied any size of ball and off he went at great speed to grab hold of it or kick it. Even as a baby he often toddled around in his baby walker with a wooden spoon in one hand leaning over the side of the walker and batting at a tennis ball. As he got older it was football, rugby, tennis or golf. He loved all games that involved a ball. When Kyle got his hand on his golf club or tennis racket it was advisable to keep your distance. Although they were plastic, he could still inflict quite a lot of pain to anyone who happened to get within striking distance.

He had good fun with his rugby ball for he could line it up, take a few steps back and then run and kick for goal as good as any professional. This was often followed by a laugh and a cheer. He also had to carry a towel with his tennis racket and after batting a few balls he would stop and wipe the handle of his racket. Obviously he had been watching too much Wimbledon.

Kyle loved playing outside as well as indoors with his ball. Therefore, we had to make sure the back garden was very secure. On a couple of occasions the garden gate was inadvertently left open and Kyle got out giving me a real fright. He never did develop any road sense. Once, when he was about six years old, he escaped out of the garden and ventured onto the main road. Thankfully, a careful and considerate motorist stopped her car and took Kyle to Moira's house, our neighbour across the road, to where Kyle had been heading. Previously Kyle and I had visited Moira many times, but on this occasion he had decided to venture over on his own. Meanwhile, back home I was just about going frantic running around the house and garden searching everywhere for him. I was greatly relieved when I spied Moira bringing little Kyle back by the hand. As usual he was laughing, obviously he had enjoyed his little adventure but was totally unaware of my anxiety and his danger. That episode gave us an extreme fright and thereafter we were constantly telling our other two boys and their friends to make sure they shut the gates when they came in or went out.

Kyle's energy levels never wavered during his many years of lack of sleep. Someone has postulated the idea that the reason why children with Sanfilippo sleep so little and are so very active in the early years of their lives is because they have so much living to fit into so few years. The hospital prescribed 'Melatonin' to help settle Kyle at night. Initially we did get a few hours sleep of and on until his body became accustomed to it. The dose then had to be increased.

It was interesting to see that Kyle always went to bed with a smile and woke up next morning with a smile. In fact, no matter what time of the night or morning Kyle wakened, be it at one, two or three o'clock in the morning, he was always full of happy giggles and bundles of energy. However exhausted I might have felt it was impossible to feel cross or be annoyed with Kyle. He made us laugh with his joyful attitude to life.

Even though Kyle had all the expected characteristics and symptoms of Sanfilippo syndrome, yet I did not see them. To me he was adorable, funny, lovable, innocent and always "my wee man", a gift to treasure and never a burden.

Probably the worst thing to cope with through those years was that Kyle could not tell us what was upsetting him when he was in pain. He was usually such a happy little boy as he demonstrated by smiling and giggling in the middle of the night just as much as he did in the daytime. We knew that if Kyle was upset or crying there had to be a reason. When this happened a visit to the doctor usually proved it was an ear infection. Kyle had vents inserted when he had his tonsils removed at the end of September 1997. The situation improved considerably following this surgery and the number of infections was greatly diminished. When the doctor was unable to find a reason for what was upsetting Kyle we then had to visit the dentist to eliminate any dental explanation for the hurt.

At one stage Kyle was fitted with a hearing aid due to him suffering slight hearing loss. However, it became impossible and impracticable as we were forever losing the hearing aid, even though we had it etched with Kyle's name and our home phone number. When we found it and replaced it in Kyle's ear he would soon remove it again and fling it somewhere out of sight. We decided that trying to keep the hearing aid was not worth the aggravation.

I remember Kyle being quite upset one day when he arrived home from school in the taxi. The driver was a little embarrassed, but neither the driver nor I knew what had caused Kyle to be so tearful. It was only the following day that I discovered the reason for the tears. When I looked into the back of the taxi I saw that another little boy had Kyle by the hair and was pulling as hard as he could. Soon after that Kyle began to travel to school on a bus with an escort on board. This alleviated a lot of the transport problems.

When I look back and recall the years of mass destruction in our home I have to smile and wonder how I coped. The fact that I was a little bit younger then probably helped quite a bit. During those years I not only had more energy, but lived with the awareness that Kyle would not always be as active because of his deteriorating condition. This awareness always helped me find that last ounce of patience to deal with many trying and difficult situations. My sisters used to say that as we got older I was always the most easy-going out of the three of us for I was never easily riled. What annoyed them most was that they could rarely get me into an argument or have me take sides with either one of them. I was always the peacemaker.

However, with Kyle I do recall feeling totally overwhelmed on occasions. My way of coping was to secure Kyle into his buggy and just walk the roads of Kilkeel to get a break and enjoy the fresh air and sea breezes. This helped to relieve the pressure and frustration. I had always found it difficult to share my deepest feelings with other people, but found that as I walked I would recite Psalms and talk with God. I shared with Him all my worries, my troubles and all my fears about the future. As I poured out my heart to God I realised that prayer was the shortest route between my heart and His. As I off-loaded my burdens on the Lord, in return He filled my heart with His peace.

After these walks with God I would return home quite refreshed. I found a lot of comfort in the Psalms of David. They were of great value for teaching me to praise God through trying times. I can still remember on one such walk I was so thankful to God that at least Kyle was still able to cause havoc and had not yet lost much ground to this incurable disease. The Psalms also gave us a lot of guidance and encouragement to trust God when we could not understand what was happening or foresee what lay ahead of us. Psalm 147:3-5 assured us that "He healeth the broken in heart, and bindeth up their wounds. He telleth the number of the stars; He calleth them all by their names. Great is our Lord, and of great power; His understanding is infinite." I found it amazing to read that God, who is far greater than the universe He created, cared about me, our family and about our sorrows. He was neither remote nor aloof from us, but close at hand with love and mercy for His people. He was bringing healing to our deeply-wounded spirits. From creating the world and naming the stars, He now gave attention to mending our hearts. Nothing is too hard for Him.

"Spiritual victory is a day to day relying on Jesus Christ" (Alison's Journal).

8

Going To School

It was a big day for us when Kyle got his "statement of special educational needs" from the Education Board. This enabled him to commence school in September 1997. It was recommended that Kyle should attend Rathfriland Hill School (now Rathore School) in Newry. This was a new and challenging threshold for us and principally for Kyle, but we were not sure how it would go. I remembered that our previous experiences at 'play school' had been disastrous. However, after Andrew and I paid a visit to the school we were more than happy for Kyle to start his school career there.

When the day finally arrived for his first day at school he looked so grown up in his black trousers and red jumper. I could not help but notice that Kyle was not only wearing a different uniform from his brothers, but that he was also going to attend a different type of school. Nevertheless, I had to be positive and assure myself that this was what was best for Kyle. We really wanted a school that would be able to accommodate Kyle throughout all stages of his degenerative disorder to avoid the disruption of having to move from one school to another during the process.

It was a great relief to us to find that Kyle really did enjoy his first week at school. Of course, the other side to that happy transition was the excellent work of the staff and teachers at Rathfriland Hill School who made school such an enjoyable experience for Kyle. We will always be grateful for all they did for our wee Kyle.

Every morning Kyle stood at the window waiting for the school bus to collect him. When the bus did arrive he never knew whether he should remain standing at the window laughing at the bus or go out and get on it. He never seemed to learn the routine. The driver was always very cordial and adept in welcoming Kyle and the other children aboard.

The school organised various special events for the children and took them on many class outings. These days out were captured on camera and we have some wonderful pictures of Kyle and his friends on these trips. In one photo he was dressed as a Red Indian, no doubt his usual bizarre antics justified that snapshot. There was another picture of him winning a prize on a "mad hair day", again a very appropriate award for Kyle. In yet another photo Kyle looked totally relaxed with his feet immersed in a foot spa. Now that was a unique moment for Kyle who never seemed to relax during his waking hours. When I look at the excitement and happiness on the faces of the children I sometimes wish school had been like that for us.

When Kyle returned home from school every day he had a notebook which documented all that he had been doing that day. The report also raised any concerns that his teachers or carers might have had about him. His very first annual school report read, "A very happy boy, and although a challenge for the staff during the past year, we have all thoroughly enjoyed watching Kyle." We were so pleased.

Over the years we built up a very close relationship with Rathore School and all those involved with Kyle. It was very evident that their main interest was to make life better for Kyle and his friends.

Soon after Kyle was diagnosed with Sanfilippo we were assigned a social worker who was able to advise us regarding respite care. This was something we had never considered. Initially, I had great difficulty in even thinking about letting Kyle go anywhere without us. To hand our son over to the care and attention of others, at first made me feel as though I was failing my son in some way. I felt I needed to care for him myself.

However, we were invited to send Kyle to Orana Respite Unit in Newry for a respite period. This was not only a big step for Kyle, it was for me too and I had to break myself in gradually. At the start we left him for an hour while we went shopping in Newry. Kyle seemed to really enjoy his hours at the unit where the staff were most helpful and the facilities excellent.

Gradually we were able to extend the length of time Kyle spent at the unit until he was able to manage his first overnight stay, which I still remember so well. I could not even bear the thought of taking him to Newry for an overnight stay. I had to let Andrew and his Mum take him to the Orana Respite Unit while I sat at home and cried my eyes out. I felt I was a failure besides feeling so guilty at letting him go. After he had gone I felt even worse for not being able to take him to Newry myself.

As was typical, Kyle took to the new surroundings at the Unit like a duck to water and had not a care in the world while I moped at home. I felt greatly rebuked. Little by little I was able to accept the situation and began to realise that this allowed me to spend more time with Craig and Scott and give them more attention.

After I was able to adjust to the Respite Unit visits, we were all able to benefit from Kyle's respite for approximately two nights each month. This allowed us to spend some quality time with Craig and Scott. Andrew and I were able to do things with them and go places together where we just could not have taken Kyle. During the summer the Orana Unit was able to keep Kyle for extended periods and this allowed the four of us to have a family holiday. This certainly gave us all a much needed break, time to recharge the batteries and get caught up on some sleep.

For all the disruption in their lives, Craig and Scott never complained. On the contrary, they were quick to show their love, care and consideration to Kyle. During the early years of Kyle's illness it was very difficult trying to help Craig and Scott with their homework. Kyle was forever lifting their school books or grabbing their pencils and often managed to scribble on many of their homework books. We only solved this problem when we had Kyle's room completed for his exclusive use.

Like all children, Craig and Scott had their favourite toys. However, playing with them and preserving them was not easy. When they wanted to play with Lego, Kyle tended to demolish everything they built and the boys always had to look out for flying missiles when Kyle took to flinging into the air whatever he got his hands on.

Like all mothers, I wanted to be the perfect mum to all of my children, but at times I felt so frustrated. I tried to juggle my time between caring for Kyle and at the same time giving due attention to Craig and Scott. Owing to hospital visits, doctors' appointments and dental engagements, it was not always easy to find time for everything I wanted to do. Furthermore, having my time and energy monopolized by Kyle often left me totally drained and not able to give the other two boys the attention they needed. Just trying to accomplish simple tasks like keeping on top of the household chores became very annoying. I finally had to accept that if the house was not vacuumed or the windows washed, it did not really matter.

When Craig and Scott were younger, Andrew and I would take turns on Saturday mornings to go with one of them into town for a treat at the local café. This enabled us to spend time with each of the boys individually in the hope that they would not feel left out or neglected.

Kyle's illness and the resultant difficult behaviour restricted us from enjoying many family pursuits that other families were able to take for granted. I remember asking Craig and Scott when they were a little older if they ever felt they had missed out on anything while they were growing up seeing Mum and Dad had to spend so much time with Kyle. They both gave an emphatic 'No'. They maintained that they never ever felt left out or disadvantaged in any way. They loved Kyle very much and nothing was ever a problem when it came to doing something for him or with him.

Kyle was as much part of Craig and Scott's life as he was of ours.

"We do not need to see the way ahead as long as we stay close to the One who does" (Alison's Journal).

9

On The Move

In December 2001 we moved house after living at Cranfield for almost fifteen years. We were thankful to God for His provision. For several years we tried to accommodate Kyle's increasing disability, and put in plans to adapt our home accordingly, but we just seemed to hit one hurdle after another.

Andrew's mother, Bertha Shields, lived next door to us at Cranfield. She willingly agreed with us to sell both houses and build one new home, which would be suitable to accommodate all our needs. Of course, this move meant that we were transferring away from the seaside, but the new site had a beautiful panoramic view of the Mourne Mountains and was still very near to Kilkeel.

The move worked out very well for all of us. We designed the house so that Bertha was able to maintain her independence with her own kitchen, lounge, bathroom, bedroom and separate entrance to the house. We were able to custom design our living area to meet Kyle's and our family needs, yet all this under the same roof. This also meant that we were all near at hand if we needed Nannie or she needed us. Craig and Scott enjoyed the added benefit of Nannie always being conveniently available for a cuppa and a chat when Mum was busy with Kyle.

We built the new home with Kyle uppermost in our minds. His room was fitted with an overhead hoist that ran straight through to his bathroom, which was complete with a Jacuzzi, which he greatly loved. We had a camera installed in Kyle's room so we could monitor him on any television in the house.

The money for this close-circuit television was donated by the Wednesday Support Group, which I attended when possible. This group of ladies, who meet weekly for tea and fellowship, come from different churches in Kilkeel. Many of them have known tragic circumstances in their own lives. Their warmth, love and friendship were and still are a great help and encouragement to me.

Kyle had a multi-sensory station provided by "Make a Wish Foundation"; a wonderful organisation dedicated to fulfilling the wishes of terminally ill children. Kyle thoroughly enjoyed this equipment which consisted of a large beanbag with speakers enclosed. When connected to a hi-fi the beanbag vibrated with the rhythm of the music. Besides having fibre optic strands which Kyle enjoyed clutching with his hands, the station also had a bubble tube which Kyle loved to watch as it changed colours. This station gave Kyle untold hours of enjoyment and amusement. This was initially suggested by Breige who had nursed Kyle through Hospice, at home and later became Kyle's community children's nurse. Breige was very much part of the family and we appreciate all the care and love that she demonstrated to Kyle.

In our previous home Kyle's room was adapted for his safety. In our new home Kyle's room became more like a hospital ward and was fully equipped with oxygen cylinders, suction machine, nebuliser, hoists, feeding pump, all his syringes, nappies, medicines and the rest of his medical supplies.

We experienced yet another move in 2001. When Horizon House

KYLE
6 WEEKS OLD

ONE WEEK OLD.
WITH SCOTT
& CRAIG

Kyle's
PHOTO ALBUM

FAMILY PHOTO,
AUGUST 1993

KYLE 10 MONTHS OLD

First steps!
CHRISTMAS 1993

OCTOBER 1993

Potty training!

WHERE'S MY BALL?

Three men in a tub!

Kyle with his big brothers

MAY 1994

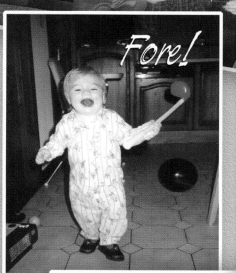

Fore!

Keep out!

**ALMOST 2,
SEPTEMBER 1994**

Fun & games

Sporting allrounder!

SCHOOL OUTING

FOOTBALL . . .

TENNIS . . .

ENJOYING A FOOT SPA

RUGBY

GOING FOR A SPIN!

BIG CHIEF!

PC KYLE

SCHOOL DAYS

Having a good chuckle!

SEPTEMBER 2004

Enjoying a dip!

New school uniform

KYLE WITH SCOTT & CRAIG.
MARCH 2006

KYLE AT HOME

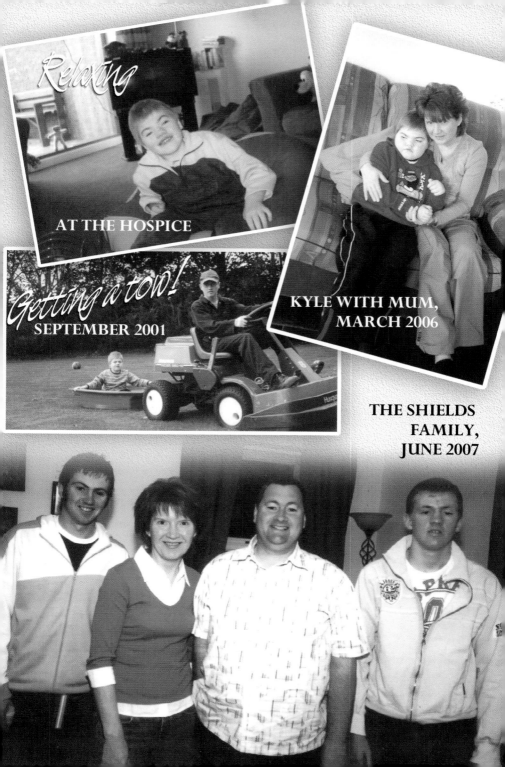

Relaxing
AT THE HOSPICE

Getting a tow!
SEPTEMBER 2001

KYLE WITH MUM,
MARCH 2006

THE SHIELDS
FAMILY,
JUNE 2007

Kyle

EARLY 2003

(Northern Ireland's only Children's Hospice) opened in Belfast in October 2001, it was a great blessing for many families, including ours. When I first heard of the Hospice I automatically thought of palliative care for children suffering from cancer. For me this sounded too much like a depressing place where children went to die. How wrong I was. I was pleasantly surprised to discover that the Children's Hospice provided care and support for children with a wide range of life-limiting, or life-threatening conditions. They also provide care and assistance for the families of these children, from the moment of diagnosis onwards.

Besides providing palliative and terminal care, Horizon House also provides specialised respite service, practical advice and assistance as well as bereavement support for as long as might be necessary. We discovered that they also offer a Hospice-at-home service, whereby some of their nurses go out to attend and care for children in their own homes.

Horizon House, situated at the edge of Belfast in Newtownabbey, with beautiful views overlooking Belfast Lough, was nothing like the dreary place I had imagined it would be. On the contrary, it is a bright, homely place which often resonates with laughter from the children having a jolly good time. The mission of the Children's Hospice is to improve the quality of life for the whole family and we know that they accomplish their mission admirably.

The facilities at Horizon House are outstanding. In addition to the purpose-built children's accommodation, they have family rooms, art and music rooms, a multi-sensory room, play area and a hydrotherapy pool. The care team includes nurses, doctors, physiotherapists, care assistants, social workers, chaplains and specialist therapists, all of whom are very caring and really dedicated to their work.

Kyle was one of the first children to use the facilities of Horizon House where he was in his element playing with his ball and running up and down the spacious corridor. For the last five years of Kyle's life the Hospice became an extended part of our home. On many occasions not only did Andrew and I stay at Horizon House, but Craig and Scott were also able to make use of the overnight facilities.

As a result of the one-to-one care during these latter years we were able to build close friendships with many of the Hospice care team. I have to mention Rachel for she was Kyle's special nurse. Rachel also looked on Kyle as her 'wee man'. I used to laugh when the girls said they were not as concerned about telling me if Kyle had fallen or had hurt himself. They were more worried about telling Rachel and how she would react. It was lovely for us that Rachel was able to visit Kyle at our home too and look after him in his normal at-home surroundings.

Compliments must also go to Joe the Hospice chef. Not only was the Hospice food excellent, but Joe's scones were gorgeous. You have not really lived until you have tasted Joe's delectable home-made scones.

The biggest drawback for us using the facilities at Horizon House was the distance. It is an hour and a half drive from our home in Kilkeel to Newtownabbey. So many families from all over Northern Ireland were in need of the unit and this meant that availability of respite was often quite limited.

As Kyle's condition deteriorated and his nursing needs became more demanding his proportion of respite time increased. Kyle was usually offered a placement in the unit when any cancellations occurred.

Visiting the Hospice helped me to keep things in perspective. Every time I went there I became aware of other families who were in far more complex and difficult situations than we were. This always made me thankful for all that our family had. We treasure many very precious memories of Kyle at Horizon House and that facility will always have a very special place in our hearts.

In 1996 the Young Married Couples' Group in our church, Kilkeel Baptist Tabernacle, were asked to conduct the Young People's Fellowship meeting one Sunday evening. For that meeting the group decided they would offer a singing item. Four married couples, including Andrew and I, volunteered to sing. We really enjoyed the fellowship on the night that we met for the rehearsal and concluded that we should get together more often like that. Furthermore, the meeting went so well that we were invited to sing at our own Sunday evening Church service.

Following those small beginnings we were invited to sing again at our own church on different occasions and even received invitations to sing at other churches. When it became evident the singing group had unwittingly become established we thought it would be better if we had a name. Since most of us in the group had been through various difficult times and had proved the Lord's strength and nearness, we decided to call the singing group 'Immanuel' (God with us).

God has truly been with us and we can thank Him for His faithfulness to the group and in our individual lives. On the Sunday evening following Kyle's diagnosis we were due to sing in our own Church. One of the pieces we had chosen was called, "It's Been Done". The song starts by saying, "We will never have to suffer. We will never have to cry." We were not able to sing that night. As far as I was concerned I was suffering and I was crying and there was no way I could face it. The words of the verse actually say;

"We will never have to suffer,
We will never have to cry
Like the Saviour did on Calvary,
On the cross He bled and died"

How true those words are, even though I could not sing them that night. No matter how much suffering we may go through in this life, it is nothing compared to what our Saviour did for us. In giving His life on Calvary's cross "It was all for me, Yes, all for me, Such love of God shown on Calvary".

So many of the pieces we sing have special meaning to us. The songs not only testify to the fact that "We Stand Redeemed" because of Christ's atoning sacrifice on "A Hill Called Mount Calvary". Our songs also remind us that "We Have a Source of Strength When We Are Weak" and He will hear our cry and keep us safe "Till the Storm Passes By".

We have really been blessed as we have travelled around Northern Ireland singing and testifying for the Saviour. We praise God for His help and guidance. In October 2003 we launched a CD and tape which we simply named, "Immanuel". The Hospice was able to accommodate Kyle so that Andrew and I could both be free to attend the launch of the CD. The date of the launch coincided with Kyle's eleventh birthday. While in the Hospice one of the children presented Kyle with a £1 coin in a little box as a birthday present. That pound was never spent for we regarded it much to precious to spend and it still remains in its box today. That CD proved to be a great success and from the proceeds we were able to donate a lot of money to missionary friends around the world.

As Kyle's health deteriorated I had to refrain from singing with the group because I did not want to leave him. At the same time, I have been strengthened and encouraged as I have been assured of the prayers of lots of God's people in the various churches where we have sung. I am grateful to all our friends in "Immanuel" for their loyal friendship, great encouragement, constant love and their ready shoulder to cry on through many trying days.

During the difficult years since Kyle had been diagnosed, our friends, Gordon and Elizabeth Bell, Alan and Jillian McConnell, Glyn and Heidi Lucas have been towers of strength to Andrew and me. They have truly empathised with us, demonstrated their care, their prayer, their practical love and thoughtfulness to us. I will never be able to adequately express just how grateful we are to all of them. Thank you 'Immanuel'.

"Immanuel"

"A true friend is one who comes in when all the world has gone out" (Alison's Journal).

10

Slow Down

It had been heart rending to watch our young son slowly go downhill over the years. Seeing him slowly lose his faculties one by one seemed to me like the toll of a dull bell ringing his approaching death. We helplessly watched as he lost his ability to speak. Even though this ability to articulate words disappeared Kyle could still be quite vocal. He made himself understood by making lots of sounds that were not recognisable as words. We knew what he meant.

Kyle's ability to run and jump began to slowly decline until he even lost all capacity to walk on his own. This deterioration happened so gradually that it was hard to put a specific date or age when he went off his feet. As his muscles began to waste he became more and more unsteady on his feet and would fall quite easily and more frequently.

On one occasion Kyle fell against our kitchen worktop and broke part of his front tooth. This resulted in a long trip to the South Tyrone Hospital in Dungannon, as that was the only place available for an early appointment. Thankfully, Eunice, whose navigational skills are greater than mine, was available to drive to the unit.

Initially, as Kyle's condition slowly worsened we did everything to try and support him as he tried his best to walk. Kyle loved to be on his feet and would start to giggle the minute his feet touched the floor. However, from around his twelfth birthday his wee legs just could not support him any more. From that point onwards he had to use his buggy or chair constantly to move around.

Ironically, this meant he was no longer the uncontrollable child he once was. No longer did we see him as our little hurricane who would dart off at lightening speed in any direction or clear the entire breakfast bar with one swipe of his hand. Those years of chaos had flown by and we had come to a very definite transitional time.

During the eight years since Kyle had been diagnosed we had experienced every human emotion imaginable. We had gone through devastation, hopelessness, despair and denial. We had also learned to accept the unexpected, be prepared for everything and never take a good day for granted. Most of all, we made up our minds to enjoy every moment of our precious son's time with us.

In many ways things were a little bit calmer in our home now that Kyle was immobile. This was the first time that I was really able to enjoy nursing and cuddling him. Previously he was always too busy to be cuddled and never had time to sit on anyone's knee. Furthermore, we now had arrived at the stage where Kyle's nursing needs began to greatly increase.

Since Kyle was no longer mobile he had to be frequently moved to prevent pressure ulcers. This involved a lot more handling. Rather than hoisting Kyle with the apparatus provided I tended to lift Kyle. Lifting in this way would definitely not be recommended by any occupational therapist or physiotherapist. However, I found it was quicker, easier and a lot less hassle. In addition, I felt it gave me a lot more intimate and personal involvement with Kyle.

On the evening of April 12th 2003 I got Kyle settled to sleep and went upstairs to bed as usual. As always, I switched on the monitor so we could hear Kyle in his room downstairs. I was unable to sleep that night for I could hear him gabbling away in the early hours. Just as I had done on almost every night I went downstairs again to try and settle him for some sleep. I found he had soiled his nappy. I was just about to put on the fresh nappy when he suddenly went into a seizure. It never even occurred to me to panic or phone for a doctor. From some First Aid training I had received in my distant past I knew to turn him on to his side and monitor him. Immediately after he came out of the seizure he fell into a deep sleep, so I just sat with him for the rest of the night and did not phone his GP until the morning.

I think the doctor was quite surprised that I had not phoned him during the night. He told me that Kyle could not be started on any medication until after he had a second seizure. I was then given advice on dealing with epilepsy.

From that night onwards Kyle was never left on his own. Thereafter, I was not even able to hang clothes out or take a shower without someone being present to keep an eye on Kyle. During this time we were grateful for the additional benefit of having Andrew's Mum living under the same roof. When needed, she kept an eye on Kyle for a few minutes while I attended to some chore.

Kyle was still attending Rathore School in Newry so I tried to get everything done during the day while he was at school. On the night after he had his seizure I moved a bed into Kyle's room. Previously I had been content to use the monitor in our room, but now I was worried that I might not hear what was happening in his room.

He had his second seizure twelve days after the first and again, it was during the night. Initially, most of his seizures occurred during the night. The second seizure lasted longer than the first. Remembering what the doctor had said, I phoned for an ambulance and Kyle was admitted to Daisy Hill Hospital. He was immediately started on a drug called Epilium. In addition, I was given Diazepam enemas to be administered to him rectally in case he suffered prolonged seizures.

After Kyle's second seizure others followed frequently and without any regular pattern. He might have had a seizure on two or three consecutive days and then none for about a week only to suffer two or three more on the same day. Some of these attacks lasted less than a minute and at other times he needed the Diazepam enema to help bring him round.

After three years, in May 2006, the hospital changed his medication for epilepsy from Diazepam to Midazolam. We found this medicine not only had a better effect on Kyle, but it also could be given orally, onto his gums. I cannot explain why, it might have been maternal instinct, but I could always tell that a seizure was about to happen a few seconds before it actually did. I cannot identify any specific reason for this intuition, but on numerous occasions I would waken, jump out of bed and rush over to Kyle, knowing that he was about to have a seizure.

As the situation worsened and the epileptic seizures became more frequent, my mum started to stay with Kyle one night each week. This enabled me to catch up on some sleep, although, at my request, she knew to always call me in the event of an attack.

Through time and much practice, we learned to cope well with Kyle's seizures at home. He only ever needed to be admitted to hospital for his epilepsy once more. That was on 22nd December 2005 when Kyle's epileptic seizure lasted for more than twenty minutes. Although we administered oxygen and gave him Diazepam he still did not respond. His breathing became much more laboured and his heart rate began to soar. On that dark wintry night with the countryside sparkling with Christmas decorations we had another speedy ambulance ride to Daisy Hill Hospital. The trip proved to be a bit difficult because of the Christmas shoppers in Newry being out in force. The driver had to skilfully weave his way in and out through the traffic to get us to the hospital quickly. Although the ambulance was going as fast as possible, in the back of the ambulance with our extremely ill son, it seemed as though we would never arrive.

The medical staff managed to get Kyle stabilised during the night and on the next day he was discharged home. In retrospect we are glad that he was home for Christmas. We did not realise then, but this was to be Kyle's last Christmas here on earth.

Although I had read that many children with Sanfilippo have epilepsy in the final stages of the disease, it still came as a shock to us. Kyle was only ten years old when the epilepsy first started. As far as I was concerned, he was not near the final stages of his life yet. We had been told that Kyle would have a life expectancy of about fourteen years, but I was always sure that Kyle would be the exception and would be one of those children who would be able to make it into his late teens or early twenties.

Since Kyle's slowing down was happening gradually we did not really pay much attention to it, nor were we really aware of it. Epileptic seizures were something we could not ignore, but I thought we were coping. Many times I asked how I could deal with Kyle's epilepsy or how to learn to live with the terrible pain of watching our darling child shuddering and jolting uncontrollably in these seizures. All loving parents can identify with this same feeling. When our children hurt, parents also hurt. When the pain went on and on without any respite, there never seemed to be any answer or meaning to our heartaches.

As Christians, we found it comforting to realise that God was not a Spectator in our troubled lives. He was a Participant, a very present help in all times of affliction. Whatever hurts us touches Him. God cares about our cares and also cares for us. Like Asaph, in Psalm 93, I discovered that as I walked through the dark days of life I was not alone. There is no greater source of comfort or courage than to know that God will never leave me nor forsake me. Asaph's most wonderful discovery was that God's presence, strength and wisdom would never end. Just to know that God had not forgotten or abandoned us was an amazing source of strength for us.

Asaph concluded that God was in control even when he suffered and did not understand why he was suffering. Through these years of trial I gained the confident assurance that even when life seems unfair, God will always be fair. The circumstances in which we found ourselves did not diminish God's goodness. The Bible does not promise believers a life free of pain, difficulties or loss, but grace for each trial and light for the way.

As a Christian, I must not expect to be exempt from struggles, heartache and disappointments, but I do have the assurance of a Companion and Friend to help, strengthen, encourage and guide me in whatever comes my way. One wise old saint said, "You never know Jesus is all you need until Jesus is all you've got." How true that is!

"God may send me a burden but He never overburdens me. My problems can never exhaust His provisions" (Alison's Journal).

11

Our Daily Bread

Towards the end of 2003 Kyle began to have more problems with eating. Until then, he had managed to sustain a pretty normal diet; he loved his mashed potatoes and gravy, yoghurts and custard cream biscuits. Now, however, he started to have problems swallowing his food. This meant it took us longer and longer to feed Kyle, even though his food was liquidized. He began to cough and splutter over his juice and other liquids so that it became difficult for him to take his medications. It seemed as though he was spitting out just as much as he swallowed.

The inability to swallow concerned me greatly for it seemed to compound Kyle's struggle with epilepsy. What worried me most was that he was having more frequent fits and I could not be sure if it was because he was not getting his proper doses of medication. To make matters worse, Kyle had also lost such a lot of weight. It was decided by the doctors at hospital that he should have a videofluoroscopy to access his swallow. This procedure involved Kyle swallowing some radio-opaque fluid that could be observed as he swallowed, similar to an x-ray in motion.

This procedure was undertaken in April 2004 and it identified a problem of aspiration creating a high risk of Kyle's food going into his lungs rather than into his stomach. It was, therefore, recommended that alternative feeding methods should be urgently considered. Kyle was still attending the Orana Respite Unit at that time, but once they learned of the result of the videofluoroscopy they requested a risk assessment be completed.

Initially, our social worker did not foresee any problems in this request and duly completed the risk assessment, which was to be presented at Kyle's review on 15th June 2004. We were totally shocked at the review when we were told that Kyle could no longer attend the Orana Respite Unit because his nursing needs had become too substantial for them to cope with safely.

What complicated matters further was that we had already booked our annual family holiday for July and we were depending on Kyle being able to spend those two weeks in the Orana Unit. Yet again I left another meeting in floods of tears when I was told by the chairperson of the meeting, quite insensitively and uncaringly I felt, that the holiday company would probably refund our money under the circumstances. It was not the compensation that troubled us, but the insensitive dismissal and another rebuff for Kyle's situation.

The Hospice nurse who had attended the review took me across the road for a cup of tea and gave me a shoulder to cry on. I was so grateful when the Hospice staff kindly offered to step in and accommodate Kyle for five of the nights. When my big sister, Wilma, sorry, older sister, who was still living in Derbyshire, heard of our predicament she decided to take leave from her nursing post to fly over to Kilkeel to keep Kyle for the remainder of the two weeks.

By Wilma coming over to allow us to have a family holiday she set a precedent for she would do the same during the summers of 2005 and 2006. We will always be grateful to her as it gave us the confidence to be able to go off to relax, soak up the sun and recharge our batteries knowing that Kyle was being cared for by very capable and loving hands. Wilma said that she felt privileged to be able to look after Kyle as it allowed her to spend some time with her nephew and get to know him better since she was not able to visit us as often as she would have liked.

Four months after undergoing the videofluoroscopy Kyle was admitted to the Royal Belfast Children's Hospital in preparation for his operation the following day to help alleviate his swallowing problem. This involved Kyle having a general anaesthetic and putting a feeding tube directly into his stomach via the abdomen.

I had a great mental battle and a real conflict of emotions about this operation. I had been waiting for this day since the result of his videofluoroscopy in April, but I knew that children could sometimes become too weak to undergo the surgery. With each month that passed Kyle struggled more and more to swallow his food and I was worried that the hospital might be leaving it too late for the surgery. Every mealtime lasted up to an hour during which Kyle coughed and spluttered with each mouthful. It was painful to watch my wee boy just wearing himself out in the effort to have some sustenance.

I was quite apprehensive, not only because of the actual operation, but I was concerned about how I would cope with caring for the wound site and administering his feeding regime. These anxieties were tempered with the fact that Kyle really needed the operation in order to provide a sustainable method that would enable him to obtain his food, fluids and medications safely.

Kyle was assigned to a bed in the middle of the ward, just across from the nurses' station. His named nurse went through all Kyle's details such as height, weight, allergies, medication, previous operations, in-patient stays etc. As a frequent hospital visitor I was already prepared for this and had everything listed. Kyle was soon moved to his own side ward that had a large adjacent bathroom with shower. There was also a folding bed, which enabled me to stay beside Kyle at night.

The side room was a lot quieter than the open ward and had plenty of room for Kyle to use his buggy and enjoy the other toys he had brought. However, Kyle was to have another dreaded blood test. The doctor informed me just after eight o'clock in the evening that Kyle's platelets were dangerously low and, therefore, he needed to do another blood test to double check that it would be safe enough for Kyle to undergo an operation. With a low platelet count there was no way they would operate because Kyle's blood would be slow to clot and therefore, increased the risk of haemorrhage.

I was devastated at the possibility of a postponement to the operation. Kyle needed his gastronomy tube to be able to get his essential nutrients. I dreaded the thought of having to return home only to have to come back at a later date. To face another hospital admission would have been a traumatic experience for both of us.

With Kyle's blood test in mind, I telephoned a few friends and asked them to pray for the situation. When the doctor came to take blood from Kyle, he applied the 'magic cream' to dull the pain and after three attempts with a syringe, he finally got some blood.

About an hour later I was told that the blood sample was fine and that Kyle would be first in line for theatre the next morning. This was a real answer to prayer. Not only were my fears and forebodings of having to return home lifted, but I had to laugh when the nursing assistant brought in a full dinner for Kyle before he began fasting for the operation. There must have been a lack of communication somewhere for there was no way Kyle could have eaten such a large meal. If he had been able to eat such a meal he would not have needed the operation.

Kyle, oblivious of what was ahead of him, had quite a good sleep that night and only wakened a few times. In the morning he was wheeled down to theatre in his bed from which he was lifted over onto the operating table. The anaesthetist put him under with gas and I had to give him a tearful goodbye kiss, and return to the side ward and wait.

Following the operation Kyle was taken to the recovery ward and remained there for quite some time as his temperature and blood pressure were both extremely low. I was allowed to be with him during this time so I kept vigil at his bedside.

Over the next couple of days Kyle slowly recovered, although he did have several epileptic seizures while there. After moving out of the recovery unit we spent another three nights in hospital before we were allowed to bring Kyle home at the end of the week. Those days in hospital after his operation gave me an opportunity to become familiar with Kyle's feeding programme. I had to learn how to look after his wound site where the tube entered into his stomach just below his umbilicus.

Through this procedure I was reminded that we often learn quickly by our mistakes. Kyle tended to wriggle around frequently in bed during the night. On our second night at home I managed to spill most of Kyle's feed over the bed because one of the valves had become detached. The feed, which resembled very milky cold tea, made such a mess over everything. Kyle always loved to hold something with his hands, so the feeding tube exiting from his tummy was as good as anything else. After finding him with his tube pulled taut several times, I managed to find some baby teething rings and Kyle was quite content to hold these instead of the tube. I soon became more confident and proficient in managing Kyle's feeds to the point that I was even amazed at how quickly I had adapted to this new routine in Kyle's life.

Within a few weeks of his operation Kyle began to gain weight and have fewer seizures. Receiving all his essential nutrients and medications via the PEG (the feeding tube) made a great difference to Kyle.

I remember in the earlier years of Kyle's condition, reading about how the disease would progress and wondering how I would ever cope when Kyle got to those stages. *How would I cope with tube feeding, with epileptic seizures and twenty-four hour nursing care?* Now, as I analysed the situation, I realised we had reached that stage and we were coping quite well. Of course, along the way I did have many weepy moments. We did not cease to be human. At times we seemed to stagger from one hurdle to another and from one crisis to another, but I'm so thankful that we had the Lord to help us over all those hurdles and emergencies.

What I found very difficult to handle was that at my age, when most parents were enjoying seeing their children develop and starting to become more independent, I still seemed to be spending more and more time familiarising myself with the inside of the various hospitals. At times I wondered how things might have been had Kyle been born without this syndrome. I only wished that he did not have to suffer from this dreadful disease. At the same time, I was also conscious that if we had not come through this experience we would never have proved the goodness of God in so many wonderful ways. For that very reason we are thankful to God that He sent Kyle to our home and for all the pleasure that our wee son brought us. Through it all God's grace has been sufficient, our faith in Him has been strengthened and even in the darkest hours of our midnight experience when I was at my weakest and no one saw me, knew or understood what I was going through, the Lord was there. He knew, He cared and He gave me the strength to carry on.

I proved the truth contained in this poem:

It's in the Valleys I grow

Sometimes life seems hard to bear,
Full of sorrow, trouble and woe
It's then I have to remember
That it's in the valleys I grow.

If I always stayed on the mountain top
And never experienced pain,
I would never appreciate God's love
And would be living in vain.

I have so much to learn
And my growth is very slow,
Sometimes I need the mountaintops,
But it's in the valleys I grow.

I do not understand
Why things happen as they do,
But I am sure of this one thing.
My Lord will see me through.

My little valleys are nothing
When I picture Christ on the cross
He went through the valley of death;
His victory was Satan's loss.

Forgive me Lord, for complaining
When I'm feeling so very low.
Just give me a gentle reminder
That it's in the valleys I grow.

Continue to strengthen me, Lord
And use my life each day
To share your love with others
And help them find their way.

Thank you for valleys, Lord
For this one thing I know
The mountaintops are glorious
But it's in the valleys I grow!

"When God is in control of our lives, nothing happens by accident" (Alison's Journal).

12

Those Who Cared

As Kyle's nursing needs became more substantial we were able to secure some assistance at home. Initially Sylvia and Virginia attended to Kyle's needs. Although they were Kyle's carers they became more like part of our family. Their love and devotion to Kyle was very evident in their treatment and care of him. Sylvia, as well as assisting with bathing and preparing Kyle for bed, took over from my Mum in spending a night each week with Kyle. Like any teenager, Kyle was still growing and this meant Mum was finding him increasingly difficult to manage on her own. Virginia came to look after Kyle on alternate Saturday afternoons. This enabled me to attend to shopping and other chores at home.

When Kyle's condition continued to decline the Newry and Mourne Community Children's Nursing Team came on the scene and made themselves available to offer support and advice. This support included nurses, a physiotherapist, an occupational therapist and carers to look after Kyle at home. Gillian, Kyle's physiotherapist, made herself available night and day and was always on hand to give him much needed chest physiotherapy as his condition worsened.

During Kyle's final few months at home we were offered additional support for the night sits, plus extra respite and nursing care since Kyle was no longer well enough to attend school. Initially, it seemed very strange having so many people turning up at various times throughout the day. There seemed to be a constant flow of traffic coming to and going from our home, but I did not mind this invasion. On the contrary, we were very grateful for all their support and professional help. We tried to encourage all of these visitors to make themselves right at home in our house, but it must not have been easy for them caring for a child while his Mum was hovering around in the background.

We got to know all the nurses really well. They just came and went like part of the family and Kyle just loved all the attention they showered upon him. Those nurses who stayed through the night arrived at 11.00 pm and stayed until 7.00am. Craig and Scott seemed to be amused by all the comings and goings and used to ask "Who's coming tonight?"

I think they just wanted to know who they would be meeting next morning when they came downstairs just after 6.00am for breakfast. So many visitors never seemed to bother the two boys and we always encouraged them to continue to bring their friends to our house in spite of the increased traffic. We were glad that they did so and neither they nor their friends ever seemed to be embarrassed about having to cope with a disabled brother.

When Kyle was first diagnosed with Sanfilippo he was the only child living in Northern Ireland known to have the syndrome, although there were other children who had other MPS diseases (e.g. Hunters, Hurlers and Morquio). Since then, at least four other children in Northern Ireland have been diagnosed with Sanfilippo.

As the occasion arose, we were able to be in contact with a family from just outside Coleraine whose daughter, Jade, was diagnosed with Sanfilippo. Although they live at the opposite end of the country, we have managed to meet up with them several times and also to talk on the phone. When I was over visiting my sister, Wilma, in England, I had the privilege of visiting a family near Leicester who have two children with Sanfilippo.

In those days just after Kyle was diagnosed, Wilma's brother-in-law said that he was sure there was a family in the church he previously attended before moving, who had children with the same disease. That was how the contact was established with the Donegani family in Leicester. We found it good to talk with people who really understood and knew just what we were going through.

Though there were times when I thought that no one understood what we were facing, it was good to know that we have a Heavenly Father who knows just what we are going through. It was so comforting to know that He saw the hurt we had inside and was always there when we needed Him. All we had to do was call on Him, "Let us therefore come boldly unto the throne of grace, that we may obtain mercy, and find grace to help in time of need" (Hebrews 4:16).

The words of the following song are very appropriate:

MY FATHER KNOWS
Are there things inside your heart you think no one understands?
Do you smile and face them on your own?
And when it's late at night and there's no one else around
Does your smile disappear when you're alone?

Chorus
My Father knows just what you're going through,
My Father knows He's reaching out to you
And there's no need to run from Him
He loves you, so come to Him my Father knows.

There's no need to run away 'cause you cannot hide from Him
For He sees the hurt you have inside,
And when no one seems to care or even understand
He is always there, in Him you can confide.

The Donegani family in Leicester shared a lovely poem with me:

"I Refuse"

I refuse to be discouraged, though I'm often sad and cry.
I refuse to be downhearted, and here's the reason why,
I have a God who's mighty, Who's sovereign and supreme,
I have a God who loves me, and I am on His team.

He is all wise and powerful; Jesus is His name,
Though everything is changeable, my God remains the same.
God knows all that's happening, beginning to the end.
His presence is my comfort. He is my dearest friend.

When sickness comes to weaken, and bring my head down low,
I call upon my mighty God, into His arms I go.
When circumstances threaten to rob me of my peace,
He draws me close unto His breast, where all my strivings cease.

When my heart melts within me, and weakness takes control,
He gathers me into His arms. He soothes my heart and soul.
The great "I AM" is with me. My life is in His hands
The "Son of God", He is my hope. It's in His strength I stand.

I refuse to be defeated. My eyes are on my God,
He has promised to be with me, as through this life I trod.
I'm looking past my circumstances, to Heaven's throne above.
My prayers have reached the heart of God. I'm resting in His love.
I give thanks in everything. My eyes are on His face.
The battle's His, the victory mine; He'll help me run the race.
I can do all things through Christ who strengthens me!

"To show His love for me Jesus Christ died for me. To show my love for Christ I must live for Him" (Alison's Journal).

13

Thirteen and Counting

I was not sure why I was feeling a bit fearful when we entered into the New Year of 2006. I do not know if it was because Kyle had been in hospital just prior to Christmas with another seizure and I was beginning to realise that he was not as well as he had been previously. It might have been because I knew Kyle would become fourteen years old in October 2006 and we had been told by the doctors that his life expectancy was about fourteen years.

I remember so well that first Sunday of the New Year. Pastor Alan Dundas spoke on Deuteronomy 31:6; "Be strong and of good courage, fear not nor be afraid of them, for the Lord thy God, He it is who doth go with thee, He will not fail thee, nor forsake thee."

On the way out of church I commented to Alan that his message had been for me that morning. It was exactly what I needed and I claimed the verse for the year ahead of us. It was probably just as well that I did not truly realise what the days ahead would bring.

Kyle started the New Year with a chest infection and on another antibiotic. Over the next months he would have fourteen courses of antibiotics for he just seemed to have one chest infection after another and each time it was taking two or three courses of an antibiotic to clear up the infections.

This takes me back to the beginning of this story when Andrew had gone to Ballykelly with Craig and Scott for the motocross event. It was on Easter Monday, 17th April 2006, the day before my birthday, when Andrew phoned in the afternoon to tell me that he was in Altnagelvin hospital with Craig who had a suspected broken leg.

My immediate reaction was that I wanted to be there. Imagination is often worse than reality and mine began to run riot. I needed to see Craig and make sure he was all right. However, I had to organize care for Kyle before I could go anywhere. Andrew rang back later to say that Craig's left femur was fractured and he would be going to theatre on the following day, Tuesday, to have the femur pinned.

I phoned the Hospice and they, ever willing to help, said they could keep Kyle from Wednesday onwards. I organized for Sylvia to sit with Kyle on the Tuesday evening. Meanwhile, Andrew had driven the whole way home from Londonderry to take me back to see Craig. I'm not sure how he managed it as it was at least a five hour round trip in the heavy Easter traffic.

We arrived at the hospital on Tuesday evening and I felt better when I saw Craig. We were greeted with the news that a pressing emergency had been admitted to the hospital and Craig's operation had been put back until the Wednesday. I was taken aback to find Craig quite agitated and some of his conversation was a bit confused and bizarre. However, after speaking with the nurses it appeared that this behaviour was due to the morphine they had given Craig to help control his pain.

We returned to Kilkeel that night feeling somewhat happier with the situation and thinking that after his surgery on the following morning we would soon see Craig on the way to recovery.

Andrew and Scott went back to work on Wednesday so my Mum and

Dad offered to take me to Londonderry. We expected Craig to be in theatre in the morning and assuming that he would still be quite drowsy from the anaesthetic, we decided to travel to Newtownabbey first and take Kyle to the Hospice. Kyle was now at a stage where I did not like to drive with him long distances on my own. If he needed repositioning or had a seizure while I was driving there would be no way of stopping the car immediately and attending to him. Therefore, someone always had to travel with us or we went with them.

It was late afternoon by the time we got to the hospital. The nurse on the ward informed us that Craig was still in theatre and could be still there for quite a while. I presumed that he had gone to theatre later than had been initially planned. Since it was a long journey to and from Londonderry, I told Mum and Dad to go on home as Craig would likely sleep the rest of the evening. I planned to sit and wait in the ward for him to return.

About an hour later the surgeon came in to tell me that Craig was being taken to the Intensive Care Unit (ICU) and someone would be along to take me down once they got him settled in. I could hardly take it in. *"This was not meant to happen,"* I thought. I was shell-shocked and numb. No one could have predicted this happening.

The surgeon explained to me that Craig had developed a fat embolism. Once they put the monitors on him in theatre they realised he was not getting enough oxygen. This was because fat from his bone marrow had infiltrated into his blood stream and caused an embolism in his lungs. The surgeon further explained that because of this they were not able to proceed with surgery as they would not want to risk disturbing more bone marrow. Instead, they had fitted a large external fixation device to immobilise Craig's femur. The surgeon assured me that once Craig was well enough he would be back in theatre to have this fixator removed and the pin put into the bone as planned.

On reading up on fat embolism afterwards I read that it occurs mostly in young men with long bone fractures. Prompt surgical stabilisation of such fractures, like that performed on Craig, is done to reduce the risk of an embolism. Some of the symptoms of the presence of an embolism include shortness of breath, restlessness, fever, high pulse rate and a confused state. That was exactly what we had witnessed with Craig when I arrived on Easter Tuesday evening.

I was really upset when I thought about Craig being in ICU and was probably a bit frightened too. I immediately phoned Andrew. When he heard the latest news he left home straightaway to come to the hospital. Pastor Dundas and our good friend Gordon Bell also travelled up to Londonderry to give us support at this anxious time.

When I got into the ICU I found Craig was hooked up to monitors and an oxygen mask covering his face. He was able to respond to me, but was still very confused and agitated. I noticed he had developed a rash. The nurse explained to me that the rash was another symptom of the fat embolism.

I remained overnight with Craig in ICU while Andrew went to stay nearby with kind friends, John and Elizabeth McCormick. We had not known John and Elizabeth previously, but Pastor Dundas introduced us to them and when they learned of our predicament they immediately offered us the use of their home while Craig was in Altnagelvin Hospital.

John and Elizabeth's hospitality was limitless. They gave us the keys to their house and encouraged us to come and go as we wanted. Besides being so helpful to us, they also offered accommodation to my sister, Wilma, when she flew over from England to support us at this difficult time. Elizabeth also prepared a meal for us each evening and for any friends who came from Kilkeel to visit Craig and us. A friend back home expressed some concern that I might be neglecting myself, but I was able to tell her that I was eating better in Londonderry than if I had been at home. John and Elizabeth's love, care and consideration were overwhelming and this kindly couple will long be remembered for their real Christian hospitality.

On Thursday Craig's condition remained unchanged. He continued to maintain his oxygen levels while he used the oxygen mask, but he was still as "high as a kite". Whether this was because of the morphine or the embolism we will never know, but poor Craig had not a clue what he was saying and to this very day he does not remember a thing about it.

When Dad and Pastor Dundas came up to visit again, Craig kept us all entertained by the things he was saying. He spoke seriously of selling his scrambler machine and buying a big American fridge full of Sukie Juice to put in his bedroom from which he would never come out again.

Craig's favourite nurse was Debbie who according to him in his delirious state "was the only nurse in the hospital who knew anything," and she would be getting the biggest pay rise ever after he had spoken to her boss. "After all," he insisted, "the amount of money that footballers got was ridiculous money for what they did compared to Debbie." Maybe Craig was not as delirious as we thought and had a valid point!

At other times Craig became quite agitated because his oxygen mask was irritating him. When we failed to understand what he was trying to say he became very frustrated. On several occasions he said he saw men at the window. According to Craig they were holding big sticks and were coming to beat him up. He was so terrified of these imaginary men that no amount of reassurance from us seemed to alleviate these fears. In the evenings Craig was quite content for me to go back to the McCormick's home as he had Nurse Debbie to look after him and protect him during the night.

We thought we might be at John and Elizabeth's home for about a week, but more unforeseen setbacks lay ahead of us. Early on the following morning I returned to ICU and sat by Craig's bed where I read my devotions for that day. My Bible reading for that day was in 2 Samuel 12. I did not think too much about what I had read at the time as my mind was racing ahead about other things. Later on that morning, just for a change of position, I went down to the hospital canteen for a cup of tea. While there I texted a few friends and family to let them know that Craig seemed to be doing well. I also reported to them about Craig's antics and the great *'craic'* we had enjoyed with him on the night before.

It is strange how things can change so suddenly and without any warning. When I got back to ICU Craig's oxygen levels had dropped dramatically and he was struggling to breathe even with the oxygen mask. The nurse on duty ushered Andrew and me to the family room as they prepared to put Craig onto a life support machine. They told us that the doctor would come to speak to us once they got him stabilised.

I found that Intensive Care Units were peculiar places, especially the family room. There always seemed to be families and people there, everyone waiting for news, but unsure if it would be good news or bad news, yet they were hoping and praying for the best. People filed in and out of the waiting room in pairs as only two people were allowed at an ICU bedside at any one time.

Newspapers and magazines lay scattered on the coffee table beside a few half-empty cups and the remains of some leftover food. Evidently, anxiety meant that most of the food was hardly touched and would soon be in the litter bins. The television was blaring, but no one seemed particularly interested, they just watched idly without paying much attention. On one occasion, while I was anxiously waiting I glanced up at the television and noticed that an episode of the drama "Casualty" was showing a hospital emergency room. I found this most disturbing in the midst of our crisis and asked someone if they minded my switching to another channel.

Most people in these waiting rooms had their mobile phones at the ready, sending texts or making phone calls to keep people informed of the latest developments. At times there was small talk between the different families. Most were aware of each others' situation and how their loved one was progressing, but generally, each family was wrapped up in their own concerns and anxieties.

As we sat in the family room waiting for what seemed like an eternity I recalled what I had been reading in 2 Samuel 12 earlier that morning. Verses twenty-two and twenty-three of that chapter particularly struck me. David said, "While the child was yet alive, I fasted and wept, for I said, who can tell whether God will be gracious to me that the child may live. But now he is dead, why should I fast? Can I bring him back again? I shall go to him, but he shall not return to me." When I remembered these words I panicked. My initial thoughts were, *"God, what are You trying to say to me? You cannot mean that you are going to take Craig? Yes, I'm prepared for You to take Kyle* (or so I thought) *who has been so ill for so long, but not Craig, Lord.'* I just could not get my head around this. My thoughts were all over the place and nothing seemed to be making any sense.

I was never so glad to see the Pastor coming to visit us on that day. He talked with us, read the Scriptures and prayed with us. He just seemed to have the right words I needed to hear at that time. Like Queen Esther in the Bible, God definitely had sent Alan Dundas to us for "such a time as this."

As long as Craig was still alive I knew that there was still hope. He was brave and was a fighter. We continued to pray that God would be gracious and spare him. I can honestly say I truly cried out to God and never prayed before as much as I did during those few days.

The doctor emerged some time later and ushered the other families out of the waiting area so that he could speak to us privately. He began to explain that Craig was now on a ventilator. He told us what to expect and gave details of where various tubes were. He was obviously preparing us for seeing Craig so that we would not be too shocked.

It was not easy to look at our eldest son lying in the bed, heavily sedated and not able to do anything for himself. What was even more frustrating was that we, his Mum and Dad, could do nothing to help him. Even a machine was doing the breathing for him. How grateful I am for God's strength which is made perfect in my weakness. I can truly testify that "God was *my* refuge and strength, a very present help in trouble" (Psalm 46:1). This verse became very real to us and a great encouragement to hope and trust in God, in His power and providence through which He would strengthen us.

Pastor Dundas stayed at John and Elizabeth's home with us that night. I really wanted to stay over night at the hospital for I hated the idea of leaving Craig lying there, looking so vulnerable and obviously so very ill. However, I was encouraged to go to the McCormicks' home for I needed a good night's rest or else I would not be of use to anyone the following day. The nursing staff promised to phone us if there was any change in Craig's condition during the night and since the McCormick's home was so nearby, I agreed to follow their advice. Although I didn't sleep much, at least I got a rest and a change of position.

Saturday saw Craig's condition remain unchanged. It was a very long day to be just sitting at his bedside or in the family room. We had been waiting and watching throughout the day while various family members came to visit us.

When there was a changeover of nursing shifts we were not allowed into the ICU. During this time Andrew and I took the opportunity to pop out to the local shop and purchase a few toiletries. It seemed so surreal that everyone could be wrapped up in their shopping while our world was falling apart. I felt like shouting at them, "Don't you realise what's happening in my life? Don't you care that my son is so ill?" We quickly bought what we needed and headed straight back to the hospital to wait for the nurses to finish their transfer procedure. I just could not get out of the shop soon enough.

Although we were not able to do anything for Craig physically, yet we never stopped praying that the Lord would intervene in the situation. On Sunday evening we were told things were beginning to look a little better for Craig. He was unconscious and although still on a life support machine, his lung x-rays showed a slight improvement.

I believe God truly was working a miracle for us in answer to many people's prayers. Our own church in Kilkeel met that Sunday afternoon to pray specifically for Craig. Many others friends across Northern Ireland and beyond were also praying for him and us.

On Tuesday, more than a week after his accident, the medical staff at the ICU were gradually able to wean Craig off the life support machine and although he was still quite confused, he was able to breathe on his own again and maintain good oxygen levels. By this time I was concerned that if his brain had been starved of oxygen his ongoing confusion might then be permanent. However, my fears were alleviated when the medical staff reassured us that the confusion persisted because of the amount of morphine that had to be administered to keep him free from pain.

On Thursday evening they were able to move Craig out of ICU and back into the orthopaedic ward. He was still in a lot of pain and was constantly pressing the self-administering morphine button to pump more pain-killer into his body. Even then, Craig was convinced that they were not giving him sufficient pain-killers. The external fixation device on his leg looked rather gruesome. It resembled a train track running alongside the outside of his thigh with four large metal pins going through the flesh and into the leg to hold the bone in position. Touching his leg or any movement of his leg was extremely painful. Craig's pain was worse when the nurses came to clean around the device. At such times he was always glad that his Mum was nearby to comfort him.

On several occasions we thought that Craig was finally going to theatre to have the pin inserted in his bone, but we were disappointed each time and told that they had no plans for surgery yet. Somehow there appeared to be a lack of communication between the hospital staff and us. It left us all frustrated for Craig who had already prepared himself mentally for surgery a couple of times.

In the back of my mind I was also thinking about Kyle, not only wondering how he was, but also, how much longer the Hospice would be able to care for him. At the same time I did not feel that I could leave Craig while he still had to go for more surgery. It was an awful dilemma. While I felt that Craig needed me more than Kyle at that time, yet I had also planned that if Kyle had to be sent home then I would have no other choice but to go home to care for him. Although Wilma had stated that she was more than willing to take time off and come over to look after Kyle, I really did not want to inconvenience her. I committed it all to the Lord and was prepared to accept whatever way things might work out. I knew the Lord did not make any mistakes and that His timing was always perfect.

Finally, on 2nd May, exactly two weeks after the original fracture, Craig was taken back to theatre in Altnagelvin to have the external fixation device removed and a pin inserted in his femur. There were concerns again that more bone marrow could be deposited in his lungs so a bed was prepared in ICU to cater for any emergency.

Craig was the first down to theatre at just after nine o'clock in the morning and was not brought back to the ward until after two o'clock in the afternoon. Thankfully the bed in ICU was not needed. We were allowed to see him in the recovery room about fifteen minutes prior to his return to the ward. I think the hospital staff realised just how traumatic the previous ten days had been for us all and were trying to reassure us.

For the next few days Craig was in severe pain and the physiotherapists were certainly not the most popular visitors. Nevertheless, he did love the constant stream of visitors and their attention. This helped cheer him up immensely and enabled him to cope with his severe pain. Considering that he was a two and a half-hour journey away from home, we felt that he must be a popular young man to receive so many visits.

This might sound unbelievable, but, on the Wednesday evening, without warning, our middle boy, Scott, appeared at the ward with a plaster of Paris on his right arm. It had still been painful since the accident he had suffered on his push bike on Easter Saturday so his cousin Trevor took him to the Accident and Emergency Department at Newtownards Hospital to have it X-rayed. They discovered that he had fractured a bone in his arm. I could not believe it. Here we had Craig in bed with a broken leg, Scott with a broken arm and Kyle being cared for in the Hospice! It felt like the Shields family were among the walking wounded except that Craig was not walking too far yet.

Besides all this, Scott was due to start his GCSE exams the following week. Unfortunately for Scott, his mishap was not a good enough reason to be excused from his exams. Therefore, it was decided by the school that he would have to dictate his answers to a classroom assistant who would do the writing for him.

On Thursday they tried to get Craig to stand on the injured leg, but he was in agony and nearly passed out. For me to be an onlooker was very difficult. I tried to rationalise and say to myself that this was essential for Craig to get up and start moving. However, my maternal instinct wanted to protect my son from any more pain and trauma. I felt as though I was torn between the physiotherapists and Craig.

By Friday he managed to stand on his own for a brief period, even though he still found it painful. On Monday, 8th May, Craig celebrated his eighteenth birthday while still in hospital. He even got mentioned that day by Hugo Duncan on BBC Radio Ulster's afternoon programme. My sister Eunice brought a birthday cake to the hospital for Craig and the hospital staff provided him with another one. Craig was also grateful when we brought him some fare from MacDonalds to celebrate his birthday. However, what really made his day was when he was told that once he could manage the stairs on crutches he would be allowed to go home.

With that incentive, Craig really did put a lot of effort into getting back on his feet. He worked through the pain barrier to get some movement back into his leg. At first he mastered how to stand on his feet, then he learned to walk again and finally he ventured going up and down the stairs. For him it was like a baby learning to walk all over again, only a lot more painful. For us it was a great relief.

Craig finally got home from hospital on Friday 12th May, the date we had originally scheduled for his eighteenth birthday party. Needless to say, it had to be postponed. When Andrew transported Craig home he had to change the habit of a lifetime and drive very slowly and carefully since Craig felt every bump on the road.

I left Londonderry earlier that day on my own en route to the Hospice to pick up Kyle. I had lunch there with the staff and caught up on all their news about Kyle. It was great to see my wee man whom I had not seen for almost four weeks. Although I had been totally involved with Craig for that time, Kyle had never been far from my thoughts and my prayers.

I was apprehensive about travelling without assistance in case Kyle became ill in the car. Thankfully, the journey home was uneventful, except for having to stop once in Newcastle when he had a bout of coughing. This was another answer to prayer.

"Only grace can transform our painful trials into glorious triumphs" (Alison's Journal).

14

Home, But For How Long?

It was so good to be back home in Kilkeel and back to my own bed, that is, the bed in Kyle's room. The Hospice had been great and they had looked after Kyle so well for the whole time that I was concentrating my attention on Craig. The fact that Kyle was able to stay so long at the Hospice was a real answer to prayer for us. A couple of children who were due to have respite in the Hospice had cancelled their bookings and this allowed the staff to accommodate Kyle for a much longer period than would normally have been possible.

Kyle was already on his second course of antibiotics for yet another chest infection and we noticed that he was very chesty again on the day after we got home. On the following day, which was Sunday, Kyle's condition became worse even though I was administering regular nebulisers and giving him chest physiotherapy. At that stage I really did not want to see another hospital for a long time. At the same time, I knew I was putting off what was inevitable despite the fact that I was hoping he would improve.

By late afternoon the wee man was finding it difficult to breathe, although he was on oxygen. I phoned my cousin's wife, Avril, who is a nurse and asked her to come over to our home to assess Kyle. This was probably another delaying tactic on my part for in the back of my mind I knew it would have to be a hospital admission, but I was trying to put off the inevitable. Avril only confirmed what we already knew. She stayed with us until the ambulance arrived. I had to accompany Kyle to Daisy Hill Hospital in Newry without Andrew who had to stay at home looking after Craig, who was still unable to do very much for himself.

After Kyle's admission to Daisy Hill he was taken to the Children's Ward where they immediately put him on an intravenous antibiotic and gave him increased oxygen. The doctor took me aside into a private ward and informed me that Kyle was very ill and things could go either way. The doctor wanted to know our wishes regarding resuscitation should Kyle experience heart failure. This came as a total shock to me and again I was completely at sea without Andrew being present. We had lived all these years with the possibility of losing Kyle, but now that he seemed to be getting closer to the end of his short life I had an overwhelming sense of helplessness. I felt this was not supposed to be happening to our wee boy. It is not how we would have written the script.

I had a tearful discussion with Andrew on the telephone. It was a difficult call and an emotional conversation, but Andrew was of the same mind as me. Together we decided not to resuscitate Kyle if he went into heart failure. I told the doctor of our decision. He agreed that our decision was best for Kyle and said that under the same circumstances, he would do the same. However, he assured me that he would do everything to make Kyle as comfortable as possible.

Andrew and I both knew that Kyle was in God's hands, as he had been during all of his short life. The Lord knew all about the decision we had made. We did not want to lose Kyle, but we knew that God's timing was perfect and that He alone knew the number of Kyle's days. If the Lord chose this as the time for Kyle to go I would just have to dig my fingernails into my faith, hold on for dear life and trust the Lord to bring our family through this ordeal.

Just then, Pastor Alan Dundas walked into the room where I was waiting. His timing throughout our anguish always seemed to be perfect. He helped me realise that our situation was not out of control, even though it humanly appeared to be so since we were shuttling from one hospital to another. Alan assured me that God was still in control, the Lord still cared and He was still ordering our daily lives.

The assurance that God was sovereign, He was still in control and allowed many puzzling and incomprehensible things to happen to us, gave me the ability and strength to keep on going. I have discovered that God is too wise to ever make mistakes, far too loving ever to be cruel and He is too faithful to ever let us down. Even when the going was tough and I felt that my suffering would never end, I had to realize that God was still at work and whatever came to us was sent by Him.

In the "Immanuel" group we sing "*I claim the Blood.*" The lyrics were very appropriate:

> *I have a source of strength when I am weak,*
> *That takes me through when life is pressing me.*
> *I have a source of power from above;*
> *I'm covered over by God's shield of love.*
>
> *I do not know how others make it through*
> *Who never go to Calvary as I do.*
> *For there's a healing and a cleansing stream that flows,*
> *With peace that only His redeemed can know.*

We felt it was better to be in the storm with Christ, than in calm waters without Him. I remembered that when we were children we used to sing, "With Christ in the vessel I can smile at the storm." Now we know that with Christ in our vessel we are not exempt from the storms.

Kyle slept on and off during that night while I lay in a chair listening to his every breath. The doctors informed me next morning that he was responding well to the treatment. As the week progressed Kyle continued to improve each day. Rathore School, where Kyle was a pupil, was near to Daisy Hill Hospital and it was great that the teachers and therapists from the school were able to nip in and out of the hospital to visit him.

Kyle finished his intravenous antibiotic on Friday and I was overjoyed when the doctors suggested I could take him home again providing I felt I was able to care for him. They acknowledged that there was nothing more they could do for Kyle. I had no hesitation in making up my mind about taking our wee man home and I was out through the hospital door in a shot with Kyle in his chair.

It is true that every cloud has a silver lining. Spending a week at Daisy Hill Hospital with Kyle turned out to be of benefit to Craig. Without his Mum at home to lift and lay him, he was forced to do things for himself. This helped speed up Craig's recovery as it encouraged him to do more than he otherwise might have done. He knew it was going to be a long and tedious haul to regain his strength. He was initially told that his recovery would be slow and it would likely be between nine months and a year before he would be able to return to work. Craig worked hard at his therapy and was very pleased when he managed to start back at his job in September, just six months after his near fatal accident.

Although he did sell the motorcycle on which he had crashed he did buy a replacement bike and not the big American fridge he had spoken of in hospital. I would have much preferred he had bought the latter!

Within a short time of gaining his mobility Craig was back practising his manoeuvres on his new motorcycle and could not wait for the new motocross season to start. I realize that I cannot wrap my sons in cotton wool and therefore, I placed all three boys in God's hands remembering again that the Lord is ultimately and fully in control.

"Nothing lies beyond the reach of prayer except that which lies outside the will of God" (Alison's Journal).

15

Summer Is Here Again

We returned home from Daisy Hill Hospital and Kyle had a good two weeks free from infection continuing to improve. After our being alarmed about his impending demise, we were glad when he was able to return to school within a remarkably short time. We had a lot to be thankful for.

Looking back now I can see the goodness of God in sparing Kyle's fragile life at that time. I was at an extremely low emotional, mental and physical ebb having just returned home following Craig's episode in hospital. Having to cope with Kyle's death at that time would have been unimaginable and would have left us totally drained.

I am sure the Lord would have given me the strength to continue as He had done in all the situations I have faced over the years. However, I am grateful that in His graciousness, He restored Kyle to us for a little longer.

After spending so many weeks hanging around the various hospitals we were glad when things began to get back to some form of normality. Very soon we were engrossed in a very busy few weeks, as was usual at that time of year. We had singing engagements with the "Immanuel" group, there was the Ladies' outing from our church, a Senior Citizens' outing was organised and I had always assisted with the monthly catering for the Senior Citizens meeting when Kyle's health permitted. Besides the annual church barbecue, which was soon due, we would also be marking my Nana McConnell's ninety-second birthday and we had the rescheduled eighteenth birthday party for Craig. To cope with all this we had the added complication of finding someone to care for Kyle. We wondered if it would be possible to find appropriate sitters for Kyle or if it would be necessary for Andrew or me to stay at home during these events.

Craig's birthday party was a great success and went off with a bang. I think this was to make up for the lost time during his horrendous experience when he almost lost his life. It really was a special night. Seventy-five people turned up at our home on the 2nd June to wish Craig well. His guest list kept growing longer and longer as he remembered everyone who had been so good to him when he had been ill.

During the celebration a Hospice nurse came to care for Kyle in our home. Craig continued to regain his strength and we were thankful to God for protecting and healing him. He was glad to return to work and then it was a big blessing to us when he was baptized later in the year. I do believe that the Lord used Craig's traumatic experience at Ballykelly and the awful aftermath to make him stop and think about spiritual things.

Just prior to Craig's birthday bash, Kyle was started on another antibiotic for his recurring chest infection. He responded well to the treatment. However, by the last week in June he became ill again and had to drop out of school.

We were due to fly out to Spain on the 8th July 2006, but I was beginning to think that we would have to cancel our holiday. After his third antibiotic Kyle recovered sufficiently for us to be able to go ahead with our plans. As in previous years, my sister, Wilma, flew over from England to care for Kyle whose general condition remained quite good while she was here.

Wilma jested that she had threatened Kyle that he had better stay well while his Mum and Dad were away. Jesting or not, whatever Wilma did, it obviously worked well for this was the first time I had left Kyle thinking that something might happen to him while we were away. For that reason I said to Wilma that she should contact us if anything should happen or if he suddenly deteriorated while we were in Spain. I am sure Wilma was fed up with us phoning every other day to check on Kyle. We were thankful that all went so well and that we also had a time of needed relaxation and refreshment after an exhausting few months.

After returning from Spain Kyle seemed to have continuous chest infections again. Maire, the Hospice community nurse, happened to drop into our home one day when she was in the area. I was glad to see her, but I could tell from her reaction that she was shocked by Kyle's appearance. His face had become quite puffy and fluid was beginning to gather around his ankles. She told me she thought Kyle was a very poor colour. In the conversation that followed I could see that Maire was telling me gently how poorly Kyle really was and that she thought he was in the final stages of his disease. I must have had blinkers on again for I really did not want to see, hear or digest what she was saying.

I remembered reading that denial can be a great safety valve which helps people adjust to highly emotional situations. For that reason they do not want to hear anything for which they are not ready to receive. It must have been obvious that I was not ready for what Maire was trying to tell me; I did not want to believe that we were losing our wee man. After all, we had been told earlier in the year that his death was imminent and he had survived that. Furthermore, he was not fourteen years old yet. Deep down I was clinging unto all these arguments and hoping that this was just another one of the many set backs Kyle had suffered and as on other occasions, he would soon recover again. What was more, he had already suffered from many chest infections during the course of the year and had responded to the antibiotics every time.

Maire still pressed and gently, but frankly, told me that Kyle had probably only months left rather than years. We went on to speak about resuscitation as I had done with the doctor at Daisy Hill Hospital earlier that year. I told Maire that our desire was to have Kyle at home for the end of his life. We had already pencilled Kyle in for several Hospice stays during September, October and November. Before she left I provided Maire with some additional contact details when Kyle would be at the Hospice.

During the summer the Community Children's Nursing Team was able to provide a lot of much needed respite, even though school was closed for the holidays. This was much appreciated for Nana McConnell had suddenly become very ill and I was able to spend some time with her before she passed away in Daisy Hill Hospital on 13th August 2006. Nana was ninety-two years old when the Lord took her home. She had a very long and very full life. She knew and loved her Saviour and just wanted to go to heaven and be with Him. The friends at the Hospice stepped in again to accommodate Kyle so we could attend Nana's wake and funeral.

Dr Alex Magee from the genetics team at Belfast City Hospital called at our home in early October to visit Kyle and to see if there was any advice that she could offer us. It was hard to believe that it was almost ten years since she and Dr Bell had first given us Kyle's diagnosis. In the intervening years we had met on numerous occasions and I felt it was so nice that she should take time to come to see Kyle at home. Kyle was now requiring a lot of chest physiotherapy and Gillian, the physiotherapist, came to our home daily to attend to Kyle, sometimes quite late in the evening. It got to the stage where her own young daughter asked Gillian if she was going to adopt Kyle because she felt her mother was more often at our house than at her own.

We had been invited to a wedding on Friday, 13th October and Kyle was due to go into Hospice on the Tuesday before the wedding. Dr Poots called at our house on Monday to see Kyle and when I enquired how he thought Kyle was, he told me that Kyle was a very ill little boy. He said that Kyle's colour was more grey than white. Maire and Angela from the Hospice, also called in that same day and offered an ambulance to transport Kyle to the Hospice, but I was happy that we could take him by car.

I must have been still in denial for even then I was not accepting that Kyle was dangerously ill and wondered what everybody was fussing about. Sylvia and I took Kyle to the Hospice on Tuesday afternoon, and saw him settled in. After a cup of tea and one of Joe's delicious scones we returned home.

The following morning I was getting ready for the Ladies' Support Group when I got a phone call from the Hospice. I was glad to hear that Kyle had quite a good night and although his breathing was not great, at present he was stable. I told them I would phone back after the meeting and would probably drive down to the Hospice later in the day to see Kyle.

I phoned Andrew to inform him of my plans in case he wanted to go with me after lunch. I was not able to contact him for he had already left for work. I sent him a text message in the hope that he might read it.

I had my mobile phone on silent mode during the Support Group meeting, but as I went to sit down after helping with some catering, I happened to reach into my bag to check the phone. I noticed that I had missed a call from Maire. I immediately slipped out of the meeting and phoned her. Apparently Maire had tried to phone Andrew first for she knew I would be in the meeting, but was unable to contact him so she phoned me. Maire and the Hospice staff were very concerned about Kyle and felt that we should know.

I tried to ring Andrew again, but still without success. I decided to go back home to drop Andrew's Mum off and then travel to the Hospice. I threw a few things in a bag in case I needed to stay overnight. I was just about ready to leave when Andrew arrived home. He had not felt content after receiving my phone message in the morning and had decided to come home. Seemingly, no one could contact him because he was in a bad reception area for his mobile phone.

When we arrived at the Hospice Kyle had improved a little and did not seem to be too bad. Even though he was sleeping he awakened periodically and was aware of our presence. He looked so peaceful lying in the bed, that Maire said Kyle was just making liars of them all!

We sat with Kyle all day, but even at this stage I still had not grasped that he was as poorly as the staff knew he really was. The Hospice personnel were brilliant. They provided food and cups of tea for us and our many friends and family who came to visit Kyle. They even made a beautiful collage and put it above Kyle's bed. The collage was a random collection of photos they had taken of Kyle over the years when he had been in the Hospice. They also put Kyle's hand and footprints in the centre of the collage. We thought it was so beautiful and very touching.

We were asked if it was still our wish to take Kyle home as the end approached. The Hospice staff were willing to organize an ambulance to transport him. They obviously knew that in spite of his minor improvements, Kyle's demise was imminent. However, even at this late stage I still did not fully grasp that Kyle was dying. I knew he was very ill and for that reason I did not think it would be fair to move him. I was just unwilling to accept that he was nearing the end of his short life.

Andrew and I decided against taking Kyle home. He seemed to be so comfortable at the Hospice and was being extremely well cared for. We were also receiving excellent support. We all felt at home, knew all the staff and were familiar with our surroundings. We decided that instead of going home we would stay in the Hospice parents' room that night so that we were at hand in case Kyle's condition deteriorated.

He remained stable throughout the night.

"Since our Lord may return any day, it is well to be ready to meet Him every day" (Alison's Journal).

16

The Final Day

We will never forget Scott's seventeenth birthday on Thursday 12th October 2006. Kyle slept all day at the Hospice and was very peaceful. The staff made a birthday card from Kyle with his handprints on it and this was presented to Scott later in the day. Scott still has the card in his bedroom and I am sure it is something he will always treasure.

Kyle slept peacefully throughout the morning. At one point Andrew and I were advised to go for a brief stroll in the gardens to get some fresh air and have a short break. We were only outside for several minutes when one of the staff came running towards us. She requested that we return immediately as they felt Kyle had suddenly deteriorated. In the short time it took for us to rush to Kyle's bedside he had stabilised again. Even so, it still did not register with me how extremely ill he was.

Craig, Scott, many family members and a few close friends spent most of the day with us at the Hospice. We are thankful to them for being there for their presence was such a real source of strength and encouragement to us.

Sometime during that evening, in a moment of impulse, I passed my personal journal to Pastor Dundas to read. In that journal I had kept details of Kyle's life during the past fourteen years and my reactions to the various crises. Earlier I had been reviewing the years and the different experiences I had been through with Kyle. At times it made me smile and other times to quietly weep. I did not know then that allowing Alan to see the journal would result in this book.

During the evening Valerie and Maire helped us lift Kyle out of bed and let us nurse him in our arms. My sister Eunice was on hand with her camera to capture the moment for our treasured memories. We also got photos with some of Kyle's cousins around him in his bed. Other photos were taken with various mobile phone cameras, no doubt to be retained as screen savers.

Maire went home late that afternoon, but phoned me later in the evening to see how things were with Kyle. When she heard that he was much as he had been when she left, Maire drove all the way back from Newry to be with us at the Hospice. I was surprised to meet her in the kitchen at almost midnight. Typically, she was making sandwiches for everyone. Maire's thoughtfulness, care, dedication and love, not only for Kyle, but for all our family, will always be remembered.

My sister Wilma finally arrived from England late on Thursday evening after being held up because of a cancelled flight and then another delayed flight. Kyle's condition remained unchanged so Craig and Scott travelled home with their cousin Timothy in the early hours of Friday morning. I sent them a text message about 2:30am to tell them Kyle was much the same as when they had left. They returned a text to say they had just arrived home.

At the Hospice we took it in turns to sit by Kyle while some dozed in chairs or make-shift beds in the adjacent room. The night staff slipped in and out regularly to check on Kyle and offer more tea and biscuits.

Just after 4.00 am, Wilma was sitting by Kyle's bed and I was curled up in a chair next to her, half dozing. Wilma suddenly called me. She noted that the rhythm and interval in Kyle's breathing had changed considerably with longer gaps between each breath.

By this stage Kyle's grandparents, Pastor Dundas and other family members who were still there gathered around. Kyle suddenly opened his eyes and looked at us all. He then took his last breath and slipped away peacefully. It was as if he had opened his eyes to say his final goodbye and let us know that all was well with him.

The nurse slipped in and confirmed his death at 4:10am on Friday, 13th October 2006. He sensitively offered his condolences and quietly left us to say our final goodbyes and grieve together.

I had read what someone said about grief, "If you cry a lot when you say goodbye it means you loved a lot." I did both.

Once Andrew got himself gathered together, he phoned Craig and Scott to tell them that their brother Kyle had gone home to heaven. He then called our friend Gordon and asked that he go over to our home to see Craig and Scott as we were not sure how they might have reacted to the news. Furthermore, we did not want them to be alone at that time.

Our plans for Kyle to pass away at home were not fulfilled, but we felt content that this was not meant to be. From this vantage point I can now see how it was for the best for us all. Craig and Scott will always have happy memories of the good times with Kyle at home, laughing and smiling as they entertained him.

The Lord did answer my prayers for our little son to be able to slip away peacefully with us present at his side.

I will always remember his last glance at us. That moment when he opened his eyes before he passed away to be with his Saviour will always live with me. We are so grateful to all our friends at the Hospice. Their loving support meant that Kyle's final hours and minutes were full of warmth, comfort and love. He was surrounded by his family and although his passing was devastating, it was also very serene.

"He knows each winding path I take,
And soothes each sorrow, pain and ache.
When troubles come, He's by my side,
And through them all His hand will guide"
(Alison's Journal).

17

Safe in the Arms of Jesus

We arrived home in Kilkeel just before dawn. The first place I wanted to go was to Kyle's bedroom. It was at this point that everything I knew about God, the Bible, my faith and heaven were put to the test. I needed our friends to help us and God to strengthen us as we faced Kyle's body arriving home and the wake that would follow.

For me the two days prior to the funeral passed in a haze. There was a constant procession of people passing through our home. There were lots of tears, lots of reminiscences, some laughter and many cups of tea. Through it all I could feel the Lord's sustaining hand; His grace was sufficient; His strength was holding me and He was present to help us all.

I recalled what I had noted from Psalm 138:3; " In the day when I cried thou answereth me and strengthenedst me with strength in my soul". God never disappoints us, He never fails and will never let us down. In Him I found a calm retreat as I experienced an inexplicable peace of mind and calmness of spirit through those days leading up to the funeral. It could only have come from God above.

On Friday afternoon Craig, Scott and their cousins found an old video containing clips of Kyle which were shot when he was around two or three years old which was prior to his diagnosis. There were images of Kyle playing in the back garden, kicking Craig and Scott and their cousins as they rolled about on the floor pretending to fight. We saw Kyle at Christmas with his golf club in his hands, swiping rather precariously at a ball. We watched Kyle in the paddling pool in the back garden and then in Andrew's arms at Church one Christmas morning. There were so many memories that had us laughing one moment and then sobbing the next. We revisited all those precious memories of our hyperactive little boy whose still form now lay in the casket. This went on until I had to finally ask the boys to turn the video off for they had rewound it so often that I was afraid of them wearing it out.

On the morning of Kyle's funeral I awoke quite early. I had slept very briefly during the night. I tried to pray for strength for all that lay ahead of us that day, but I could not even put a prayer together. My thoughts were on how I was ever going to make it through the day without collapsing in a heap of despair. I just cried out to God and pleaded with Him to go with me and help me through what I knew would be an extremely difficult day.

Later that morning Wilma slipped me a piece of paper which is now fixed to my journal. I read; "Fear not; for I have redeemed thee, I have called thee by thy name; thou art mine. When thou passest through the waters, I will be with thee; and through the rivers, they shall not overflow thee" (Isaiah 43:1,2). As well as being able to discuss medical issues with Wilma over the years, I also felt that in a small way she could empathise with us in what we were going through. Malcolm and Wilma had buried their first-born son, Timothy, who had died a short time after birth.

Those verses not only helped me for that moment, they also sustained me throughout the whole day. We should not be surprised when God answers our cries. I felt such a real sense of peace and God's sustaining power that can only have been found in our Lord Jesus Christ.

We were overwhelmed by the love and support shown to us by so many people. The vast number of people who attended the funeral and came from miles around was an indication to us of how much Kyle had been loved by all who knew him. Our friends from the Hospice, Orana, the MPS society, nurses, carers, therapists and some of Kyle's school friends were all in attendance.

Raymond Cassidy, Principal of Rathore School, paid the following tribute to Kyle in our home on the day of Kyle's funeral:

"Firstly I would like to say it is an honour to be here this afternoon with the Pastor, Kyle's parents, his brothers, grandparents, family members and friends.

Kyle and I started Rathfriland Hill School at the same time. From his very first day it was obvious that Kyle came from a very loving and caring family. He was a happy, carefree child who made an impression on everyone he came in contact with.

Very quickly we realised that Kyle liked running, and open doors and school corridors were irresistible. My earliest memories are of a blonde-haired boy scurrying past the office with a member of staff hot on his heels. When he had run out of corridor, he would turn around and look at the adult with a wry smile. The member of staff would ask me to have a word with Kyle - and I did. But the wry smile remained as if to say "Until the next time."

Kyle liked many things about school. He liked getting his photograph taken and over the years he has been captured on camera doing his favourite things like kicking and bouncing a ball and banging on the drums.

Kyle loved music, especially music with a good beat. Indeed his rhythm and timing were much better than most of the staff. He also enjoyed the multi-sensory room with its variety of lights and sounds. More recently his taste in music broadened and he particularly liked soft, soothing music.

With the wonderful support Kyle had from home he participated fully in school life. Who could forget his outfit on our Spanish Day when he stole the show as a waiter?

Kyle came in contact with many people within our school community - from "Big Pat" in the taxi, to his teachers, classroom assistants, pupils, governors, therapists, school secretary, caretaker and nursing team. It was with great sadness that we at Rathore convey our condolences to Kyle's family who helped him to live life to the full.

Alison and Andrew, we thank you for choosing to send Kyle to our school. It was a privilege to have known him and the whole school community will remember him."

I felt Raymond had just summed up my wee man. It was a lovely and fitting tribute to him.

There were some very difficult moments during that day. It was heartbreaking to watch my Dad, Andrew, Craig and Scott remove Kyle's coffin from our home and then carry it into the church and then carry it out again. They were also the pallbearers at the cemetery as they lowered Kyle's remains into mother earth. I ached for them as much as I was aching for myself. A mother feels the distress of all her children and it was important to me that Kyle's siblings would not be forgotten mourners.

We are very grateful and indebted to Pastor Alan Dundas for all the love, care and attention he gave to Kyle and to us during our son's final years. We are especially thankful for how he handled the funeral services, in the home, at the church and finally at the graveside. His words in each place were most appropriate, a comfort to us and a challenge to many who did not know Jesus Christ as Saviour.

Kilkeel Baptist Tabernacle was packed to capacity with family and friends for the afternoon Thanksgiving Service for the life of Kyle Thomas

William Shields. It was easy to choose the hymns for this Service for while Kyle was living I had sung them to him many times; "There's a friend for little children above the bright blue sky" and "Safe in the arms of Jesus":

Safe in the arms of Jesus, safe on His gentle breast,
There by His love o'ershaded, sweetly my soul shall rest.
Hark! 'tis the voice of angels, borne in a song to me.
Over the fields of glory, over the jasper sea.

Safe in the arms of Jesus,
Safe on His gentle breast
There by His love o'ershaded,
Sweetly my soul shall rest.

Safe in the arms of Jesus, safe from corroding care,
Safe from the world's temptations, sin cannot harm me there.
Free from the blight of sorrow, free from my doubts and fears;
Only a few more trials, only a few more tears!

Jesus, my heart's dear Refuge, Jesus has died for me;
Firm on the Rock of Ages, ever my trust shall be.
Here let me wait with patience, wait till the night is over;
Wait till I see the morning break on the golden shore.

The crowded congregation did the hymns justice as they sang with great conviction and confidence. After the first hymn the Rev. Gary Millar, the local Church of Ireland Rector, led the congregation in prayer.

In his funeral address to the church Pastor Dundas initially gave a tribute to Kyle's short life and the great assurance of the Gospel of Jesus Christ. In the course of his address in the church the Pastor paid a tribute to me for all I had done for Kyle. He referred to me as the virtuous woman of Proverbs 31:28, 29; "Her children shall rise up and call her blessed; her husband also, and he praiseth her. Many daughters have done virtuously but thou excellest them all." I felt totally unworthy, but thankfully his references to different things I had written in my journal were not just as embarrassing as these verses in Proverbs.

The Pastor's tribute made it sound as though I had been some sort of a saint and a paragon of virtue, which I definitely am not. Loving Kyle as I did was natural, easy and he was the joy of my life. I just could not have done enough for him and everything I did was only to make his short life the happiest and the best possible.

Pastor Dundas then drew our attention to 2 Kings 4:8-26 where it tells the story of a Shunammite widow who had lost her only son. She was able to say of her only son, "It is well", even though he had already died. Even though Kyle's earthly remains were contained in the coffin in front of us, it was a great comfort to be able to say of our wee Kyle "It is well with him."

Kyle was safe in the arms of Jesus. The Bible reminds us, "We sorrow not, as those who have no hope." Even though the parting here on earth was painful, yet we knew that all was well for all his sins were under the blood of our Lord Jesus Christ.

Kyle was also satisfied with the sight of the Saviour. This world could not satisfy Kyle, but now he was looking into the face of the Lord Jesus. He would be able to say with the Psalmist, "As for me, I will behold thy face in righteousness, I shall be satisfied, when I awake, with thy likeness" (Psalm 17:15).

Kyle was singing in the presence of the Lord Jesus. For Kyle the pain of this world was now long forgotten and the weakness of his body had forever gone. Kyle loved music and now he had joined the choir of heavenly voices in ascribing glory to God.

Kyle is sanctified in the arms of Jesus. According to 1 Corinthians 15:52-53 Kyle will receive a perfect body; "In a moment, in the twinkling of an eye, at the last trump: for the trumpet shall sound, and the dead shall be raised incorruptible, and we shall be changed. For this corruptible must put on incorruption, and this mortal must put on immortality."

Kyle was safe, satisfied and singing in the arms of Jesus and waiting to be sanctified on a day that is coming when he will burst forth from the grave and will receive a perfect body; "Who shall change our vile body, that it may be fashioned like unto his glorious body, according to the working whereby he is able even to subdue all things unto himself" (Philippians. 3:21).

Pastor Dundas then went on to challenge those gathered that Christ could return at any time. In the light of the imminent return of the Saviour they must trust Jesus Christ for salvation and turn from their sin to Him and ask for cleansing in the blood of Jesus Christ.

Craig had chosen the closing hymn, as it was one of his favourites and it fitted in very well with what had gone before, "There is a Redeemer, Jesus God's own Son"

I chose the following poem to be included in the hymn sheet:

> *God saw that you were getting tired.*
> *And a cure was not to be.*
> *So He wrapped His arms around you*
> *And whispered, "Come with me".*
> *Your weakened heart stopped beating,*
> *Pain free and now at rest.*
> *Although our hearts are breaking,*
> *We know God only does what's best.*

The ladies of the church provided a beautiful tea for everyone who could return to the church. This gave Andrew and me the opportunity to meet with people who had come from all over the country to sympathize with us.

Although I had many initial forebodings about the day of the funeral, yet the promise Wilma had given me that morning proved to be just the word I needed. That was the word that God used to sustain us; "When thou passest through the waters, I will be with thee; and through the rivers, they shall not overflow thee." This promise was appropriate for Peter when he was sinking midst the frenzied waves on the Sea of Galilee, but he learned the lesson that the same waters that were sweeping over his head were under His feet.

Our little family had been through deep waters of unimaginable sorrow, but we learned these waters, like the turbulent waves of Galilee, are under His feet and He was holding us. The Lord did not and will never let us go under.

"God does not comfort us to make us comfortable, but to make us comforters" (Alison's Journal).

18

Life After Shock

I need not pretend that the days immediately following Kyle's death and the months since then have all been plain sailing. We have all encountered extremely difficult days. Kyle left a huge void in our lives that can never be replaced. I just could not take it in that he would not be coming back to us. It felt as though he had just gone to Newtownabbey for respite and would be back home tomorrow, or the next day. Maybe these thoughts helped make the aching pain more bearable and was my way of coping. My loss was hurting me deeply and nothing anyone said seemed to bring any comfort to my heart.

Some well-meaning people would say, "It's better for him now"; or "He's not in any more pain." Still others would offer, "At least he's in Heaven." It sounded as though they were trying to tell us to 'chin up', but I did not find these remarks helpful. We knew that Kyle was in heaven with his Saviour and was free from all the constraints of his debilitating disease, but I still missed him sorely and would have him back if I could. The statements offered by these nice people were true, but I felt they were insensitive, sounded too clichéd and did not help me cope with the pain or the aching emptiness.

Unintentionally, people can be very hurtful with their casual comments at times of grief. Several years before Kyle passed away someone asked me if I was praying for God to take Kyle home to heaven. I was stunned to think that anyone would even consider this. I felt like asking that person if they were praying for God to take their child home to heaven. It is true that Kyle was disabled and needed twenty-four hour care, but to me, he was my very own son, our flesh and blood and therefore, no different to any other child and certainly no less loved because of his disabilities.

Somebody else recently said to me that they would not have liked to see Kyle if he had lived for another few years. Again, I think they meant well and were trying to encourage me. They were undoubtedly thinking about how much Kyle might have deteriorated. I replied that I had cared for Kyle for almost fourteen years and was prepared to continue to do so for the next fourteen, if the Lord had spared him.

During these sorrowful months I have discovered that true sympathy is not necessarily expressed by great or eloquent words. A person just putting an arm around the bereaved one and saying little or nothing is sometimes the best expression of sympathy. This gesture can say a lot more than a thousand words.

I tried to put on a public face of being strong and coping well, but inside I was in considerable turmoil. At times it felt as though no one could fully understand my sorrow. My grief seemed to be too personal; it was mine and no one else's.

Christmas came round very quickly and for us it seemed to be out of place. It was an extremely difficult time. Christmas Day was the only day in the year when all of us went to church as a family. On this first Christmas without Kyle we just could not face it. We felt that our family was incomplete for that special day. Remaining at home with other members of our wider family helped keep us occupied and diverted our thoughts somewhat.

There were days when I felt as though I was just going through the motions of living, trying to appear in control and unflappable, while underneath I was just falling apart. I tried to deal with these raw emotions and inconsolable thoughts, but they were almost too intense to bear. It seemed as though life would never be normal again. I even found it difficult to write a birthday card, an anniversary greeting or a get-well card. I still have to refrain from automatically including Kyle's name.

Perhaps one of the most upsetting adjustments is trying to get used to a silent house. There are no more of Kyle's distinctive giggles and laughter; and the constant stream of friendly carers coming and going to our door has ceased. It is almost unbearable to see Kyle's room so empty; his bed, his hoist, his feeding pump, the oxygen and all his medical supplies were all removed on the day he died. His multi-sensory station has been given to another family. Kyle's mobile and bubble tube went to Matthew, the son of a dear friend whose path I might never have crossed if it had not been for Kyle's illness.

I still feel drawn to the television monitor to watch for him. My sleep is still interrupted for I waken in the night and listen for sounds from Kyle. I then abruptly realise why I do not hear him anymore. That chubby little face, with which he looked at me, so full of trust and love, has now vanished and my words just cannot express how much I love and miss him. The excruciating pain of grief has been so sore and the longings I feel for Kyle are extremely intense. It is just like a gut-wrenching, gnawing emptiness of pain.

I found that the only way I could cope initially, was to keep busy. If I sat down to relax, my mind would then begin to wander and very soon I would be in tears.

I decided that one of the best therapies would be to go back to secular employment. After nineteen years of being at home I found returning to work was another big adjustment, but it was also a great help. It meant I was kept busy during the day and by the time I got home at night, I had the dinner to prepare, dishes to wash, make packed lunches and sort out dinner for the following day. This meant I was not only tired out at the end of the day, but the evening was almost over. I had also become accustomed over the years to making do with very little sleep. Therefore, I still find it hard to sleep at night and tend to wait until it is really late before retiring to bed.

To be truthful, I have been burning the candle at both ends to write this book, but that has not been a problem. On the contrary, it has been very beneficial to work through and reflect on all that has happened during these past years.

Life still does not feel normal when I am able to do things without having to consider Kyle. We do not have to deliberate about who will go to church and who will remain to look after our wee man. I no longer need to organize a carer so I can do my shopping or go out for an evening.

It is then that I am comforted to remember that Kyle is being better cared for by his heavenly Father.

"What we do in life echoes in eternity. That means that we have an opportunity today to make an eternal difference in the lives of others" (Alison's Journal).

19

Hope In Despair

During these days of sorrow I have laughed a bit and cried a whole lot, but this has helped me work through a lot of emotions. I have been able to take time to ponder how God has been so gracious and faithful to me in the past. The Bible reminds me that Jesus Christ is the same yesterday, today and forever. I have to accept, therefore, that life must go on and that God does not want me to be living in the past. God has a life for us after sorrow and grief.

I will never forget Kyle and there is no way that we will ever cease to miss him. I still experience those agonizing moments and bad days, but, at the same time, I am surviving without him. I know for a certainty that without Kyle I would not be the person I am today. He taught me so much and left us with a rich legacy of love. Not only did I learn the practical things such as handling his tube feeding, administering oxygen, coping with epilepsy and taking care of all his nursing needs; most importantly, I learned more about loving, understanding, patience and accepting each day as it comes. The whole experience brought us closer together as a family and deepened our bond of love and support for each other. Through the hard times, we have learned the importance of being committed to each other and the value of encouraging each other. The ten years of difficulty and adversity have only deepened our appreciation of each other.

By way of prayerful dependence on the Lord and many silent tears, I have discovered the calming peace He gives and in Him, I have found daily strength to go on. I find that when I cannot share my feelings with anyone else, I can talk to God. Prayer is the shortest route from my broken heart to His great heart. I just tell the Lord all the things I miss most about Kyle and I know He sees all my pain and is touched by my heartache. The Lord knows me better than I know myself and He always is an ever-present help in trouble.

The Bible teaches us that Christ's manhood and his priesthood make Him such a sufficient and supportive High priest; "Seeing then that we have a great high priest, that is passed into the heavens, Jesus the Son of God, let us hold fast our profession. For we have not an high priest which cannot be touched with the feeling of our infirmities; but was in all points tempted like as we are, yet without sin. Let us therefore come boldly unto the throne of grace, that we may obtain mercy, and find grace to help in time of need" (Hebrews 4:14-16). Since Jesus Christ underwent all of our human weaknesses and emotions, He, therefore, understands these same emotions and assures us that He is able to adequately undertake for us in every crisis. This means that my Lord knows when I am hurting; He sees my pain and feels my grief. He is ever near to comfort and gives me peace and hope. He loves me, sees each tear I shed and I really matter to Him.

Likewise, this sympathetic, supportive and all-sufficient Saviour also knows everything that Kyle experienced. Jesus Christ came to earth to taste death for every man, therefore, He understands death because of His own experience on the cross. He not only tasted death, but through His death and shedding of His precious blood, He triumphed over death. He, therefore, gives a full assurance to all who know Him as Saviour that sunset here on our earthly life is really a door to an eternal sunrise in a better place. We often sing, "Heaven is a wonderful place, filled with glory and grace." It is true. In that glorious land God will forever banish all suffering, pain and tears. There will be no more Sanfilippo disease.

When the troubles of this life overwhelm us like a tidal wave, we can remember that God's compassion is greater than all our grief. His love never fails and He always provides sufficient grace according to the need and difficulty of the hour. In an amazing way the Lord is able to turn our moments of weakness into times of being strong. Every day He gives me an inner strength that blossoms into outward courage. I have learned that even during the darkest nights of my experience, the morning eventually comes, a new day dawns and God sends His light when we are engulfed in darkness.

I hope that reading of our difficulties and frustrations does not give the impression that life with a Sanfilippo child is not worth living. Kyle was such a happy child and, thankfully, was oblivious to his problems. He loved to make eye contact with us and then greet us with a big smile. He used to stretch out his hand gesturing that he wanted us to hold his hand. He loved us to sing and talk to him and when we did, his whole face would light up as he started to giggle and laugh. That happy smile was a gift that Kyle shared freely; he was so precious and such a blessing to us. We are thankful that God allowed us to have him for a few short years. Our lives have been enriched because of Kyle and we have known more of the Lord's grace and goodness than we ever knew before.

Caring for Kyle brought us into contact with so many people who have become dear friends and who will always remain part of our lives. We will always be grateful to the various medical personnel, the carers and nurses who attended Kyle and us with such devotion, compassion, support and love. All these people greatly enriched our lives and made us feel special, just because of Kyle.

When I look at his photo or when I come across something in the house that belonged to him, mixed feelings swell up within me. I feel sad and tearful, yet this is accompanied with warmth and a smile. Kyle truly touched our hearts and changed our lives and will always be a part of Andrew and me. I know that the face I long to see and the hand I yearn to touch is not with us anymore, but in my thoughts the precious memories of Kyle and the years he spent with us will always be with me.

Although I would still love to have Kyle at home with us, yet we have the satisfaction of knowing that we did all we could to make his life as comfortable and enjoyable as possible. We would do it all again many times over if we could, but I have to accept that God's timing was perfect, it always is.

Today Kyle is free from his disease and with His heavenly Father. He is better off than we are. He will not only live on in our hearts and memories forever, but we will be reunited one glad day. That helps to ease my pain. I have to thank my Lord for His strength that has brought me through these years and pray for His continuing strength in the days ahead.

Amongst the many letters people kindly sent us just after Kyle's death was one from Zoë in Portadown. She included a poem. I have never met Zoë, but she was able to share in my grief for she also had lost her six-year-old daughter. The poem follows:

SUFFICIENT GRACE

Our Father is in full control of every little thing.
The sunshine and the shadows that our earthly sojourn brings;
The good days and the bad days, every trial that we face -
He has appointed it to be and offered us His grace.

BUT sometimes when the way gets rough and the darkness seems so dense,
And try as we might to understand, yet nothing makes much sense;
We struggle on the best we can, His tender voice we miss -
"Just leave your burden at My feet for I have planned all this."

It's not until we turn to Him with eyes washed by our tears,
And give to Him our storm-tossed life our worries and our fears;
That we can know the meaning of His words so warm and true -
"My grace unlimited, divine, is sufficient now for you.

"And He said unto me. My grace is sufficient for thee, for my strength is made perfect in weakness" (2 Corinthians 12:9).

Thank you Zoë. It matters to Him about you too; "Casting all your care upon him; for he careth for you" (1 Peter 5:7).

Many people die suddenly and unexpectedly. Furthermore, we do not know when the Lord Jesus will return to the earth to take believers home to heaven. It is never too early to accept the Lord Jesus Christ as Saviour, but it could be too late. I look forward to my Lord's return. He has saved me from my sin and has given me the promise of eternal life through Him.

The greatest joy on earth is the prospect of Heaven. What a reunion there is going to be up there for the Shields family.

"God's great power, provision and promises should generate our grateful praise" (Alison's Journal).